WALTER M. CAMP
Courtesy, Lilly Library, Indiana University

CUSTER AND COMPANY

Walter Camp's Notes on the
Custer Fight

Edited by
Bruce R. Liddic
and
Paul Harbaugh

*Introduction to the Bison Books Edition
by Jack D. McDermott*

UNIVERSITY OF NEBRASKA PRESS
LINCOLN AND LONDON

© 1995 by Bruce R. Liddic and Paul Harbaugh
Introduction to the Bison Books Edition © 1998 by the University of Nebraska Press
All rights reserved
⊗

First Bison Books printing: 1998
Most recent printing indicated by the last digit below:
10   9   8   7   6   5   4   3   2   1

Library of Congress Cataloging-in-Publication Data
Camp, Walter Mason, 1867–1925.
[Camp on Custer]
Custer and company: Walter Camp's notes on the Custer fight / edited by Bruce R. Liddic and Paul Harbaugh; introduction to the Bison books edition by Jack D. McDermott.
p. cm.
Originally published: Camp on Custer. Spokane, Wash.: A. H. Clark Co., 1995, in series: Hidden springs of Custeriana; 11
Includes bibliographical references and index.
ISBN 0-8032-6393-7 (pbk.: alk. paper)
1. Custer, George Armstrong, 1839–1876. 2. Little Bighorn, Battle of the, Mont., 1876. 3. Indians of North America—Wars—1866–1895. I. Liddic, Bruce R. II. Harbaugh, Paul H. III. Title.
E83.876.C15 1998
973.8′2—dc21
98-35169 CIP

Reprinted from the original 1995 edition by the Arthur H. Clark Company, Spokane WA. This Bison Books edition follows the original in beginning the preface on arabic page 11; no material has been omitted.

**For Matt and Jim
and for
Phaedra and Jerad**

Introduction to the Bison Books Edition

John D. McDermott

Born in Camptown, Pennsylvania, on April 21, 1867, Walter Mason Camp was destined to become the most knowledgeable man of his generation concerning Indian wars in the West. Generals E. A. Godfrey, Charles King, Anson Mills, and William Carey Brown named him so, and fellow researchers and collectors, such as E. A. Brininstool, W. A. Graham, and Ralph Ellison, sought his advice and companionship. Perhaps more than any other person of his era, he was responsible for rediscovering and marking battlefields where troops and tribesmen had played out the dark drama of westward expansion. His skill and dedication in commemorating the past earned him recognition as the first Honorary Companion of the Order of the Indian Wars.[1]

Camp's early interest in military matters probably came from his father, Treat Bosworth Camp. An insurance surveyor, Treat served in the Civil War as a captain of Company F, Fifty-second Pennsylvania Infantry. His ancestors had arrived in Massachusetts with the Reverend John Elliot in 1691 and fought in the Revolutionary War. Young Camp spent his boyhood in Wyalusing, Pennsylvania, where he attended public school during the winter months. At age nine he worked as a fireman in a planing mill and later found employment as a farmer and lumberman. At sixteen he became a trackwalker for the Lehigh Valley Railroad, where he learned the elements of telegraphy. In 1887 he entered Pennsylvania State College, graduating in 1891 with a degree in civil engineering.[2]

Camp spent his early career in a variety of jobs, working as a surveyor, draftsman, construction engineer, superintendent of operations, work-train foreman, and section boss for railroads in Northern California and the state of Washington. In 1895 he went back to school as a graduate student and teacher of electrical and steam engineering at the University of Wisconsin. The next year, he taught at the National School of Electricity in Chicago. Back in the railroad business in 1896, he became inspector and later superintendent of track construction for the Englewood & Chicago Railway. Finally in 1897 Camp found his life's work, becoming engineering editor of *The Railway and Engineering Review* (later *The Railway Review*), a position he held for twenty-eight years. On May 2, 1898, he married Emeline L. F. Sayles at Blue Island, Illinois. The couple did not have children.[3]

Camp soon became an authority on railway construction and maintenance and in 1903 authored *Notes on Track* in two volumes. Colleges soon adopted the study as a text. Other publications, besides his monthly column in *The Railway Review*, included numerous articles published in engineering journals, a piece on "Railroad Transportation at the Universal Exposition, St. Louis, 1904," and *Samuel Folson Patterson: An Appreciation by Members of the American Railway Bridge and Building Association* (Chicago, 1918), which he edited. His interest in the Indian wars resulted in many speeches and a few articles, most of which were summaries of campaigns rather than in-depth discussions of any particular battle.[4]

Early in life Camp became interested in Native American culture, studying several languages, including Sioux and the nearly extinct Delaware. An employee railroad pass allowed him to travel at little cost, and beginning in 1902 he spent his summer holidays visiting places in the West. Usually spending about six weeks on the road, he divided his time between locating battle sites and interviewing Indian wars participants. By his own count he visited at least forty-one battlefields. He was responsible for locating a number of battle sites that had been lost over time. One of these was the Wagon Box Fight of August 2, 1867, where Capt. James Powell and twenty-six enlisted men stood off as many as a thousand Sioux with newly acquired breechloading Springfield rifles. With Anson Mills he helped to locate the Slim Buttes site, where Gen. George Crook's troops successfully engaged the Sioux and Cheyennes in September 1876.[5]

Between 1908 and 1919 Camp interviewed almost two hundred Indian wars veterans, beginning with former Seventh Cavalry sergeant Daniel Knipe. He also recorded the stories of many Indian participants: Curley the Crow, who named him the best interviewer ever; the Cheyenne chief Two Moon; and warriors who fought against Custer, such as White Bull, Tall

Bull, He Dog, and Standing Bear. At one point Brininstool reported that Camp had interviewed every Indian still alive who had been in the Custer Fight. Not only was he a Custer buff, but his research was inclusive, embracing such other battles and campaigns as the Grattan Fight of 1854, Connor's Powder River Expedition of 1865, Red Cloud's War of 1866–68, the Battle of the Washita and the Beecher Island Fight of 1868, the Red River War of 1874, the Nez Percé War of 1877, and the Wounded Knee Tragedy of 1890.[6]

Camp's first interest, however, was the Sioux War of 1876. He had initially planned to write a history, and with this in mind he wrote Elizabeth Custer in the fall of 1908 asking for her assistance. Stating that his purpose was to write an account "that will do better justice to General Custer and the brave men under him than has yet been done," he reported that he had twice visited the Custer and Reno battlegrounds in recent years and made a survey of each with the permission of the War Department. Having the work "well in hand," he prophesied another year of research before publication and asked for an audience. His plans did not materialize, however, for in 1917 we again find him asking for a visit with Mrs. Custer for the same purpose. By this time he had interviewed more than sixty survivors of Maj. Marcus A. Reno's command, including eight officers, and more than one hundred and fifty Indian survivors.[7]

Camp discussed his own views of Custer and his role in the 1876 campaign in a letter to E. S. Godfrey in 1918. Concerning charges that Custer had disobeyed orders, Camp was clear:

> The order was a written one, and, according to my understanding of English, it was left to Custer's discretion as to whether or not he should attack should he encounter the Indians. He did encounter them, and I think he did the logical thing, as well as obeying Terry's order, in attacking them without waiting for Terry and Gibbon to come up.

Further, Camp stated that his Indian informants told him they were expecting troops to come from the north (Gibbon) or the south (Crook), because they had fought them earlier. But they were not expecting troops to appear from the east. If Custer had waited for Terry and Gibbon, Camp declared, the Indians would have seen their approach and scattered, leaving the expedition without a foe. "As to the best plan for catching up with the Indians," Camp opined, "Custer's judgment was certainly correct. The trouble was that when he did catch them he did not have men enough to handle them."[8]

Camp never did fulfill his ambition to write his history, and failing health in his last few years prohibited him from making his annual western pilgrimage. His death occurred at Kankakee, Illinois, on August 3, 1925, at the age of fifty-eight. An associate said of him, "He was the best informed man I ever knew." His obituary in *The Railway Review* characterized him as "a truly democratic man, caring nothing for the frills and fripperies of life; careless in dress, but with a friendly smile and a warm grasp of the hand for all with whom he came in contact; a real man and a real American."[9]

After Camp's death, his widow retained his files. A number of parties tried unsuccessfully to acquire them, including George Bird Grinnell, the Library of Congress, and the Department of the Army. In June 1933, after thirty-five years, Emeline finally sold most of the collection to Gen. William Carey Brown of Denver, who was financially assisted by Robert Ellison.[10] Brown was a retired general and Indian wars veteran who had commanded troops in the Sheepeater Campaign of 1879, while Ellison was a wealthy Wyoming oil executive who collected historical documents and wrote on western history.[11]

Between 1933 and 1945 Brown gradually transferred most of the files to Ellison, who was living in Colorado Springs. Ellison died on August 16, 1947, and the collection became fragmented, with pieces eventually going to the Lilly Library at Indiana University, the Denver Public Library, and Brigham Young University. The Lilly Library later received additional material from Emeline Camp's estate in 1967, and in 1986 another even smaller collection was donated to Custer Battlefield National Monument.[12] Found in this volume are interviews from another private collection. Of Camp's notes included here, those in chapters 2, 3, 4, and 6 can now be found in the Denver Public Library, while the rest remain in private hands.[13]

Contained in this volume are nineteen interviews dealing with the Sioux Campaign of 1876 and the Battle of the Little Bighorn, eighteen of them recorded by Camp. The other is a reminiscence written by Francis John Kennedy, private, Company I, which Camp copied from the Minnesota Historical Society Archives. Included are accounts of thirteen enlisted men, two scouts, two interpreters, and two Indian participants, representing many different viewpoints and perspectives. They illustrate Camp's greatest strength as a gatherer of information; he did not confine himself to one class or side but sought depth and breadth in his work.

The most extensive interview is that of Sgt. John Henley of B Troop, covering his service in the Seventh Cavalry from 1870 to 1875 and 1878 to 1883, including his participation in the 1873 Yellowstone and 1874 Black Hills Expeditions and service at Standing Rock Agency at the time of Sitting Bull's surrender. Henley had worked for a time as a trader and knew the Sioux language, allowing him to speak directly to the Huŋkpapa participants in the Battle of the Little Bighorn. Other especially valuable accounts include those of Pvts. John Lattman, Company G, and August Seifert, Company K, who fought with Reno and Captain Frederick Benteen. Taken as a whole, the nineteen accounts give us an intimate look at George Armstrong Custer and his Plains career, the men of the Seventh Cavalry, the men who fought against them, and the events that made them all famous.

In the end, Camp viewed the Indian wars as a struggle over the use of land. Mirroring the views of his day, he saw the final resolution of conflict as an object lesson—that "no people or class of men, generally speaking, shall dominate some portion of the earth if there be others who will take it and make better use of it." Camp pointed out that, although his contemporaries made much of battles, only a few tribes were at war with the United States government at any one time, and most groups had maintained peaceful and even friendly relations with white settlers. Finally, he noted that race had no monopoly on virtue—while war engendered cruelty, it occurred on all sides throughout history, and evil had no preference of color.[14] His interviews reflect an open mind and sympathetic heart, and without him we would know much less about what happened in the heat of war on the plains and prairies of the American West. To scholars he remains one of the best sources of oral information on the Indian Wars in the nineteenth century.

xii Bison Books Introduction

NOTES

1. John M. Carroll, *The Papers of the Order of Indian Wars* (Fort Collins: Old Army Press, 1975), 20.
2. Dennis Rowley and Neil Broadhurst, comps., "Biography," *The Walter Mason Camp Papers on the American Indian Wars and Custer* (Provo UT: Brigham Young University Harold Lee Library, 1981), 3.
3. "Death Comes to Walter M. Camp," *The Railway Review* 77 (8 August 1925): 208–9.
4. For examples of his general work see "Old Indian Trails," *Foreign Service Magazine* (July 1921): 5–6, and "Some of the Indian Battles and Battlefields," in Kenneth Hammer, ed., *Custer in '76: Walter Camp's Notes on the Custer Fight* (Provo UT: Brigham Young University Press, 1976), 10–25.
5. Rowley and Broadhurst, *Walter Mason Camp Papers*, 3; "Walter Mason Camp," *Railway Review* 77 (8 August 1921): 198; "Mark Graves of Forgotten Heroes," *Sheridan (WY) Press*, 29 August 1920; Hammer, *Custer in '76*, 4; William C. Brown, "The W. M. Camp Records of Indian War History," *Winners of the West* 10 (30 October 1933): 1.
6. Rowley, *The Walter Mason Camp Papers*, 3; E. A. Brininstool, letter to the editor, Los Angles CA, "The Camp-Fire," *Adventure*, p. 179, Box 23, William J. Ghent Papers, Manuscript Division, Library of Congress.
7. Camp to Elizabeth Custer, Chicago IL, 2 October 1908, Folder 19, Box 23, William J. Ghent Papers, Manuscript Division, Library of Congress; Camp to Mrs. E. B. Custer, Chicago IL, 31 October 1917, in Hammer, *Custer in '76*, 3.
8. Camp to E. S. Godfrey, Chicago IL, 18 September 1918, Folder 6, Box 24, William J. Ghent Papers, Manuscript Division, Library of Congress.
9. "Walter Mason Camp," *The Railway Review*, 197–98.
10. For details of the negotiations to obtain Camp's collection see the Grinnell-Ellison Correspondence, Brigham Young University Catalogue Number Mss/Sc/568 (microfilm, Denver Public Library); Bruce R. Liddic and Paul Harbaugh, eds., *Camp on Custer: Transcribing the Custer Myth* (Spokane WA: Arthur H. Clark, 1995), 22–25; Brown, "The W. M. Camp Records," 1; Doris Mitterling, comp., *Guide to the William Carey Brown Papers, 1854–1939* (Boulder: University of Colorado Libraries, 1978), vii.
11. William Carey Brown was born December 19, 1854, at Traverse des Sioux, Minnesota. His experience with the Indian wars began at the age of eight, when his family became fugitives during the 1862 Sioux Uprising in Minnesota. He graduated from West Point as a second lieutenant, First Cavalry, on July 3, 1877. In 1878 he fought

against the Bannocks in Oregon and the next year participated in the campaign against the Sheepeater Indians, winning a brevet for conspicuous gallantry at Big Creek, Idaho. After serving in the Spanish-American War in the Philippines, and in France in World War I, he retired on December 19, 1918. Brown died on May 8, 1939. He was the author of *The Sheepeater Campaign, 1879* (Boise: Idaho Historical Society, 1926). For a biography see George F. Brimlow, *Cavalryman Out West: Life of General William Carey Brown* (Caldwell: Caxton Printers, 1944).

Robert Spurrier Ellison was the president of the Midwest Refining Company in Casper, Wyoming. He had already published a number of historical booklets, such as *Independence Rock, The Great Register of the Desert* (1930) and *Fort Bridger, Wyoming* (1931). See "Work Achieved by Ellison in Reviving Interest in Old Landmark Recalled," *Casper Tribune-Herald*, 28 January 1936, 1; Donald E. Bower, *Fred Rosenstock, a Legend in Books and Art* (Flagstaff: Northland, 1976), 137–38.

12. Some miscellaneous materials on Camp are also found in the William Carey Brown Papers, Norlin Library, University of Colorado. See Mitterling, *Guide to the Brown Papers*.

13. Rowley and Broadhurst, *Walter Mason Camp Papers*, 8, 10–12; Bower, *Fred Rosenstock*, 138; Brown, "The W. M. Camp Records," 1; Liddic and Harbaugh, *Camp on Custer*, 27–28. Camp's interviews on the 1876 Sioux War from the Brigham Young University collections have been published in Hammer, *Custer in '76*.

14. W. M. Camp, "Some Aspects of the Indian Wars," impromptu remarks at the annual meeting of the Order of the Indian Wars, n.d., MS, Item #I-7, Papers of the Order of the Indian Wars, Military History Institute, Carlisle PA.

Table of Contents

PREFACE 11
INTRODUCTION 13

Chapter 1: Interviews with John Henley
   Biographical Introduction 31
   Interviews with John Henley 34
   The Washita Battle 36
   Yellowstone Expedition 37
   Black Hills Expedition 56
   Sitting Bull and the Battle of the Little Bighorn . . . 61
   Sitting Bull at Standing Rock 64

CHAPTER 2: 7th Cavalrymen, Frontiersmen, the Battle of the Little Bighorn and other incidents
   August Siefert 71
   John Lattman 75
   John A. Bailey 81
   Frank W. Sniffen 84
   Johnny Bruguier 87
   David McVeigh 91
   George Gaffney 93
   John Fox 94
   Thomas W. Harrison 97
   Sam Bruguier and the Capture of Rain-In-The-Face . 99
   Sam Bruguier and the Bozeman Fight 103
   Sam Bruguier and the Lame Deer Fight . . . 104
   A.W. Dale 105

CHAPTER 3: Miscellaneous Notes
   March to the Little Bighorn 107
   Regarding the Water Party 109
   Indian Strength at Little Bighorn 113

    Bradley's Scout 114
    Death of Spotted Tail 116
    White Swan 118
    Mark Kellog 119
    John Burkman 119

Chapter 4: Indian Interviews
    Thomas Disputed, Ogallala Warrior 121
    One Feather, Indian Scout 127
    Little Big Horn Indian Scouts 131

Chapter 5: The Death of Crazy Horse
    Interviews with Louis Bordeaux, Interpreter . . . 133

Chapter 6: Francis Johnson Kennedy, 7th Cavalry
    Preface 153
    Statement of Francis Johnson Kennedy 155

Chapter 7: Interview with Luther North
    Battle of Summit Springs 163
    Miscellaneous Notes 177

Index 183

Illustrations

Walter M. Camp . . . . *frontispiece*
Walter Camp and Wooden Leg 16
Robert S. Ellison 19
William C. Brown 22
John Henley 32
Sgt. Benjamin C. Criswell 35
Lt. Col. George A. Custer 57
Sitting Bull 65
Anders' Map of the Custer Battle 70
Sgt. Miles F. O'Hara 85
Captain Thomas B. Weir 95
Sgt. Thomas W. Harrison 98
Trading Post at Standing Rock Agency . . . 100
Pvt. Thomas O'Neill 108
Pvt. John Sivertsen 111
Spotted Tail 116
Touch the Clouds 134
Lt. William Philo Clark 135
Red Cloud 138
Frank Grouard 139
Fort Robinson, Nebraska 141
Red Cloud Agency Trading Post 143
Little Big Man 148
Keogh's Horse Comanche 158
Capt. Myles W. Keogh 161
Camp's Map of Summit Springs 172

Preface

It has been said that "no man is an Island." This is readily apparent when writing a book. It was in the summer of 1991 when I first saw the private collection of Walter Camp's interviews. The more I read, the more I wanted to read, and I knew that their contents needed to be shared with other Western researchers.

It took nearly a year to sort through the envelopes containing the interviews, put them into sequence, then transcribe and annotate them. Throughout this task, I have been assisted by many individuals; people who gave freely of their time and knowledge to make this book a reality. To them I owe debts that are legion and my unbounded gratitude: for my co-author Paul Harbaugh, who helped in more ways than I can recall; a thank you to R. Emmett Jordan for spending countless hours translating what passes as my handwriting into a readable page and for his many valuable suggestions which improved the book's organization; to John S. Manion and Major General Hoyt S. Vandenberg for their insight and encouragement; to Robert Aldrich for allowing extensive use of the John M. Carroll Collection; to Roger Williams, Richard "Dutch" Hardorff, Gordon Gipson, President of Caxton Printers, Ltd., Hugh E. Negus, and Sandy Barnard, a big thank you.

Not to be forgotten is my late mother who in a labor of love typed my notes several times and who willed the project to my sister, Cherry L. Hoyt, to see it finished. For the loan of rare books and articles to check the interviews against, my deepest thanks to Tom Swinford and the 'Dean' of Western bookmen, Frank L. Mercatante.

Lastly, but certainly not least, to my wife Dianne and sons Matthew and James, who endured a part-time husband and father while I worked to complete this project. With all the help and expertise I received, this should be the perfect book. If it is found lacking, the responsibility is mine alone.

BRUCE R. LIDDIC
Syracuse, New York

Introduction

Following the death of Walter Camp in 1925, Robert Ellison and General William Brown, among others, spent eight frustrating years trying to acquire the notes and interviews about the Indian Wars which Camp had recorded between 1908 and 1919. The task was Herculean, to say the least, and Ellison and Brown spent a good part of their lives first obtaining, and then cataloging Camp's papers.

In the centennial year after the Custer fight, Dr. Kenneth Hammer of the University of Wisconsin-Whitewater, edited the book *Custer in '76*, which was the first appearance in print of any part of Camp's vast collection. Prior to this, these papers were in private hands and not accessible to the general public. Book reviewers hailed the publication as "the most important source material published in a quarter century" concerning the Battle of the Little Bighorn. Those of us who are students of Americana cannot repay Camp's efforts in recording, nor Ellison's efforts in restoring to us, the information which is contained therein. In the intervening years, these Camp Notes have been used to clear up some of the mystery surrounding the Custer fight.

Walter Mason Camp (1867-1925) was a unique individual. Out of the countless students who have studied the Battle of the Little Bighorn, Camp stands alone.

Camp on Custer

He was a quiet, unassuming man engaged in an arduous quest—that of finding and interviewing every person, white or red, who survived the Little Bighorn. Armed with a tireless pen, an intense, burning interest in the Indian Wars, unbounded energy and an unlimited railroad pass, he earned a name for himself and those whom he interviewed that will live forever in the history of the Indian Wars.[1]

There was nothing in Camp's early life to indicate he would become the premier oral historian not only of Custer's Last Stand, but of all Western Indian Wars in general. He was born to Treat Bosworth Camp and Hannah A. Brown on April 21, 1867, at Camptown, Pennsylvania.[2] He received a public school education near Wyalusing, Pennsylvania. At the age of 16, he became a track walker for the Lehigh Valley Railroad, beginning a forty-two year association with railroads.[3] Camp was a highly motivated young man, and in addition to the track walking, he also learned surveying and telegraphy.

In 1887 he was admitted to Pennsylvania State College and pursued a civil engineering degree. He was graduated and started work with the Southern Pacific Company as a surveyor and later as a draftsman in the chief engineer's office. Later he was a construction engineer for the Rainier Avenue Electric Railway in Seattle, Washington. In 1894 he was employed by the Seattle Lake Shore and Eastern Railway as a train fireman. Then, after a year of post-graduate study at

---

[1] Kenneth Hammer, "Custer's Man Camp," *Manuscripts*, (Manuscript Soc., Tyler, Texas) Spring 1975, Vol. 27, #2, p. 112.
[2] Kenneth Hammer, *Custer in '76* (Provo: Brigham Young Press, 1976), p. 1.
[3] A good part of the biographical information contained here was taken from Camp's obituary which appeared in *The Railway Review* for August 8, 1925.

Introduction

the University of Wisconsin and a year of teaching at the National School of Electricity in Chicago, he became first the inspector, and then the superintendent of track construction for the Englewood and Chicago Electric Railway.

In 1897 he was appointed engineering editor of the *Railway and Engineering Review*. As editor, he:

> found the sphere of usefulness for which his talents and experience eminently fitted him, and for twenty-eight years, he served the transportation industry faithfully and well. In twenty-five years, he did not fail to produce a weekly editorial column. As a writer, Mr. Camp always commanded the respect of the railroad fraternity. He had a thorough knowledge of the practical side of railroading and knew railroad conditions and needs.[4]

Camp's only book was not about the Indian Wars and Custer, but railroad track. In 1903, his *Notes on Track*, a two-volume work, was published. It was so well received that for many years it was used as a college textbook.

How Walter Camp became interested in the Indian Wars is a mystery, but it was an all-consuming passion from the time of his first interview with 7th Cavalryman Daniel Knipe in June 1908 to his death seventeen years later.[5]

He once told Elizabeth Custer:

> I have been twenty years studying the Battle of the Little Big Horn, at leisure and irregular intervals, and have visited the battlefield nine different years, sometimes staying more than a week at a time. As to the trail between the Yellowstone and the Little Big Horn, I have been over all of it five

---
[4]Ibid, p. 197.
[5]The first interview Camp conducted was in 1908. Hammer, *Custer in '76*, p. 9.

Camp on Custer

Walter Camp and Wooden Leg, a warrior who fought Custer, taken at the Custer Battlefield in 1916.
Courtesy, Thomas Minckler Collection

Introduction

times, for the purpose of historical study, and I have been over the west end of it (between the divide and the Little Big Horn) eight times. I have interviewed more than sixty survivors of Major Reno's command including eight officers, and more than 150 Indian survivors of the Battle.[6]

When one reviews the voluminous notes and interviews, it becomes readily apparent that his greatest interest was in the Little Bighorn and the personality of George A. Custer. Most of the interviews took place between 1908 and 1919, with the vast majority done in the years before the first World War.[7]

An article in *Manuscripts* stated his methods were simple but effective:

> ...Find the desired person—Camp spared no effort and he was not easily discouraged. He once hired a horse and wagon and drove many miles of the prairies of the Dakotas to interview one Indian living at Interior, South Dakota...
> Ask the right questions—Camp knew them all. He even devised a form letter with which he gathered information by mail...
> Record the answers—Camp used any paper that was handy, including little scraps. In fact, most of his interviews were recorded on 3x5" (or smaller) slips of paper. He wrote in Pencil ... clearly and firmly in a very readable style."[8]

For a man who conducted scores of interviews, Camp never seemed to have the proper paper on his person. He would record the account on whatever scrap of paper he could obtain at the time. Some of the interviews are literally written on old envelopes, the reverse side of due bills and the back of blank preprinted forms which had been discarded. In editing this account, I noted that many of the original en-

---
[6]Ibid, p. 3.   [7]Ibid, pp. 6-9.
[8]Hammer, "Custer's Man Camp," p. 115.

velopes appeared undisturbed since the day Camp placed the contents inside. When opened, the slips of paper came tumbling out like so many snowflakes, in no particular order. I then took the slips of paper, some no bigger than a matchbook, and like a giant jigsaw puzzle, put them into a logical sequence based on their content. In trying to discover the sequence, I kept thinking of what Camp had told Colonel William Graham about the notes, "that nobody but myself would ever be able to make head or tail of them."[9]

Camp intended to take the information he had collected and write the definitive history of the Indian Wars, but as with many good intentions, he never really got started beyond a short preface.

Walter Camp was not well known outside a small circle of Western Americana experts. These people recognized his talent and knowledge for what they were and communicated with him on a regular basis. In January 1920, he addressed the Order of Indian Wars, an organization formed in 1896 to commemorate the activities of the officers and men who struggled with Indians for control of Western America. In appreciation of Camp's efforts in recording their history, he was made an Honorary Companion, the first such award ever given.[10]

Upon Camp's death, many of his friends and the experts whom he had helped and advised over the years wanted to insure his work was not lost or destroyed.[11] In fact, most of them wanted to read his interviews

---

[9]Robert M. Utley (ed.), "Recollections of Col. W.A. Graham," *Research Review*, (Journal of The Little Big Horn Associates, El Paso, Tx.) Sept. 1980, Vol. 14, #9, p. 6.

[10]John M. Carroll, *The Papers of the Order of Indian Wars* (Ft. Collins, CO: Old Army Press, 1975), pp. 20-34.

[11]Walter Camp died on August 3, 1925, in Kankakee, Illinois.

Introduction

ROBERT S. ELLISON
Courtesy, Paul Harbaugh

and study the notes he had spent nearly twenty years assembling. Again, the *Manuscripts* account is illuminating:

"... Robert S. Ellison, an avid collector of Western Americana, Brig. General William Carey Brown, and George B. Grinnell, began making overtures to the widow of Camp about Camp's papers that he had spent twenty years assembling."[12]

This was especially true for Robert S. Ellison of Casper, Wyoming. Camp and he had worked together in 1923 to locate and eventually mark the site of an Indian fight which had taken place in July of 1865.[13]

---

[12]Hammer, "Custer's Man Camp," p. 116.

[13]This fight took place on July 26, 1865, 5 miles northwest of Casper, Wyoming. It was known as "The fight at Red Buttes." For the best account of this action, see S.H. Fairchild, "The Eleventh Kansas Regiment at Platte Bridge," *Transactions* of the Kansas State Historical Society, 1904, Vol. 7.

Camp on Custer

Camp said he knew the location where the men of the 11th Kansas Cavalry were buried and directed Ellison to order the eighteen government markers and they would install them.

Two months before Walter Camp's death, he had been the guest of General William Carey Brown at the Army and Navy Club in Washington, D.C.[14] While there, Camp told both Brown and General Hugh L. Scott about their efforts to mark these graves.[15] Through the help of the two retired generals, a number of old maps were secured from the Department of the Army which Camp said would aid him in locating additional engagement sites. Both Brown and Scott were delighted that others were finally taking an interest in the history of the Indian Wars. They had felt this part of American history was being neglected or forgotten. The public's attention seemed to be focused on the recent foreign wars with Spain and Germany.

Hardly anyone was more shocked than Ellison when he learned of Camp's death. He had done as Camp had asked regarding the markers for the 11th Kansas

---

[14]William Carey Brown was born in 1854 in Minnesota. 2nd Lt. 1st Cavalry 3 July 1877. 1st Lt. 19 December 1884. Captain 6 November 1896. Graduate of Infantry and Cavalry School 1883. Major 45 U.S. Volunteers 17 August 1899. Bvt. 1st. Lt. 27 February 1890 for gallant services in action against Indians at Big Creek, Idaho, 19 August 1879. Major 23 November 1903. Lt. Colonel 1st Cavalry 11 March 1912. Retired Colonel 19 December 1918. Inspector General A.E.F., Promoted Brig. General 28 February 1927. Died 8 May 1939. Colonel William A. Powell, *List of Officers of the Army of the U.S. from 1779 to 1900* (NY: L.R. Hammerly, 1900), p. 216.

For the only biography of Brown, see George F. Brimlow, *Cavalryman Out West, Life of General William Carey Brown* (Caldwell: Caxton Printers, 1944).

[15]Hugh L. Scott was born in Danville, Kentucky, on September 22, 1853. 2nd Lt. 9th Cavalry 15 June 1876, transferred to 7th Cavalry 26 June 1876. 1st Lt. 23 June 1878. Captain 24 January 1895. Major A.A.G. Volunteers 12 May 1898. Lt. Colonel, A.A.G. Volunteers 17 August 1899. Died Washington, D.C. April 30, 1934. Powell, *List of Officers*, p. 577. For an autobiography of this soldier, see Hugh L. Scott, *Some Memories of a Soldier* (NY: n.p., 1928).

Introduction

and they had been at his home now for nearly two years. Camp was the only person who knew where to place them and Ellison, quite frankly, was getting tired of tripping over them. After waiting several months, he wrote to Walter Camp's widow Emeline and asked if she could find her husband's notes on the subject and divulge their contents. He received no reply.

On July 17, 1926, Ellison wrote to Mrs. Camp again. Four days later, she replied "[I was] unable to be of any help to you in the matter of the Indians, the reason being that the estate will not be freed from the control of the probate court until about the middle of October."[16]

Robert Ellison was frustrated. He had been storing nearly a ton of government marble for over three years and there was no end in sight. When she replied, Mrs. Camp seemed cold and distant, not wanting to be bothered. All Ellison needed was just the location information and he felt if the Army could put a little pressure on Mrs. Camp, she might supply the details her husband had recorded. Ellison took his problem to a mutual friend of both Camp and his, General William Brown.

Fortunately for the students of the Indian Wars, Brown immediately saw a much bigger picture. Of course he would use his influence with the Army to get Ellison his information, but that was only secondary. What Brown had in mind primarily was the entire Camp collection, not just a note on the 11th Kansas Cavalry. He wanted Mrs. Camp to turn over all of her husband's "Notes, papers, maps and other

---
[16]Letter, Emeline Camp to R.S. Ellison, July 21, 1926, private collection.

Camp on Custer

General William C. Brown about 1919.
Courtesy, Caxton Printers, Ltd.

records" to the War Department to be deposited in the Historical Section of the Army War College in Washington, D.C.[17]

Ellison had hit upon a real bulldog to help him, and Brown pursued the task aggressively. First he got General Charles King involved as well as two friends of the Camp family, Reverend and Mrs. Robert Ferguson.[18] Brown next contacted the Order of Indian Wars for their assistance. None of this had any effect on

---

[17]Letter, W.C. Brown to R.S. Ellison, August 24, 1927, private collection.

[18]Charles King was born in New York on 12 October 1844. U.S.M.A. 1862-1866. 1st Lt. 1st Artillery 18 June 1866. 1st Lt. 15 May 1870. Transferred to 5th Cavalry 1 January 1877. Captain 1 May 1879. Retired 14 June 1879 for disability. Brigadier General Volunteers 27 May 1898 to 15 April 1899. Died 17 March 1933 at Milwaukee, WI. Powell, *List of Officers*, p. 414.

Introduction

Mrs. Camp. 1926 turned into 1927, but Brown would not give up. He started to call in the favors he had done for his former lieutenants and captains, now colonels and generals.

He persuaded Lt. Colonel C.A. Bach, Chief of the Historical Section of the Army War College to "request his [Brown's] assistance in securing these records."[19] With this in hand, he wrote to Major General William Lassiter, Commanding Officer of the 6th Corps stationed in Chicago. Brown explained the situation in detail and asked that a staff officer from the 6th Corps "be sent to confer with Mrs. Camp" to obtain the collection, or if this was not possible, "to at least loan it to the government."[20]

While this was going on, Brown kept up a continuing correspondence with Robert Ellison. On November 10, 1927, Brown wrote that Ellison was going to be stuck with the tombstones, as he had recently discovered the remains of Sergeant Custard's detachment of the 11th Kansas Cavalry had been disinterred from their burial site in the fall of 1899 and sent for reburial at Fort D.A. Russell.[21] Brown recommended to the surprised Ellison that "a monument with names of killed and circumstances of the fight would now seem to be more appropriate than the Government headstones."[22]

Determined never to be embarrassed like this again, Ellison also threw his now considerable weight behind

---

[19] Letter, W.C. Brown to R.S. Ellison, November 5, 1927, private collection.

[20] Letter, W.C. Brown to M.G. William Lassiter, November 16, 1927, private collection.

[21] Fort D.A. Russell was a prominent post during the Indian Wars and continued right through World War II. Today it is the Francis E. Warren Air Force Base. It is located at Cheyenne, WY. Robert G. Ferris, *Soldier and Brave* (Washington, N.P.S., 1971), pp. 369-70.

[22] Letter, W.C. Brown to R.S. Ellison, November 10, 1927, private collection.

the effort to secure Camp's entire collection.[23] In the intervening years, he had been appointed Chairman of the Wyoming Historical Landmark Commission. In December of 1927, Ellison personally went to Chicago to see what could be done. Brown complained to Ellison that he had written to Mrs. Camp again, trying to set up the longed-for meeting. Brown said "were she [Mrs. Camp] a normal person, she would have replied in one way or another."[24] Needless to say, the meeting did not take place.

Brown and Ellison next heard from Lt. Colonel Bach. In effect, he told them to take it easy. In their enthusiasm to obtain the collection, the pair were ruffling a good many feathers. Bach wrote:

> I think it would be better to make haste slowly in this matter. To put too much pressure on Mrs. Camp is more than likely to give her an exaggerated idea of the value of these papers to the government ... I am stating the view that the War Department would take in the matter ... General Lassiter, working in Chicago, will undertake to secure the papers ...[25]

Brown believed that Mrs. Camp would not be able to say no to the U.S. Army and so counseled Ellison. As time would tell, Brown overestimated the ability of his military friends to deliver and underestimated the intransigence of Camp's widow. Both Brown and Ellison "backed off."

In February 1928, they learned much to their dismay that General Lassiter had been reassigned to the West

---

[23] Robert S. Ellison was at this time the Vice President of Mid-West Refining Company.
[24] Letter, W.C. Brown to R.S. Ellison, December 15, 1927, private collection.
[25] Letter, Lt. Col. C.A. Bach to W.C. Brown, December 7, 1927, private collection.

Introduction

Coast and the staff officer Lassiter had designated as his replacement replied that "... he was unable to get any satisfactory answer from Mrs. Camp and he saw no chance now of accomplishing what we want."[26]

Other people might have given up, but not Brown or Ellison. Brown said he would go to Chicago on March 1st to see personally "What could be done." Brown enlisted another friend of the Camp family, Jim Gratiot of Chicago. The combined efforts of Mr. Gratiot and Reverend Ferguson finally resulted in a meeting with Mrs. Camp. She promised:

> she would look for the papers concerning the Indian matters and let us have them.
>
> Later she reported that she had looked and could not find any ... this means I (Gratiot) have to go there and pick them out myself—that is provided she will let me, anyway that's what I am going to try to do now ... The old lady is awfully funny, though ...[27]

Gratiot also requested that since he seemed to have Mrs. Camp's confidence, whatever plans the pair had in the works to "drop them."

Mr. Gratiot replied in April 1928 that he had been to see Mrs. Camp twice more but still had no papers. He stated there "was evidence of a serious family disagreement among the members of the Camp [family] over the collection and it was wise to let things cool down a bit."[28]

By the spring of 1929, the parties began to redouble

---
[26]Letter, W.C. Brown to R.S. Ellison, February 15, 1928, private collection.
[27]Letter, J. Gratiot to R.S. Ellison, February 15, 1928, private collection.
[28]Letter, J. Gratiot to R.S. Ellison, April 14, 1928, private collection.

their efforts. So far, they had nothing to show for three years of work. In the meantime, Mrs. Camp retained a lawyer, Judd Matthews of Chicago, and on March 19th Gratiot and Ferguson met with him. Attorney Matthews listened patiently to what had prompted their visit. He replied that they could look over the papers and he would so advise Mrs. Camp. When so counseled by Matthews, Mrs. Camp replied that she had years ago mailed all the information on the battlefields to General Brown.[29] It's a small wonder Brown and Ellison did not throw up their hands and say "Enough!" Little did they realize it would be another four long, frustrating years before Mrs. Camp would finally sell her husband's papers to Brown.

It took more letters and meetings between the parties to correct Emeline Camp's belief that Brown had received any papers from her. If Brown and Ellison had thought progress was slow before, now they saw things stop altogether. The matter lay dormant until, in late 1932, with the country in the depths of the Depression, Mrs. Camp indicated she would be willing to sell the collection to these persistent gentlemen.[30]

After the sale and transfer was completed in June 1933, Brown began the difficult process of cataloging and sorting through what seemed to be an endless maze of paper pieces and the envelopes which contained them. As soon as they were classified and arranged, Brown began turning over the material to Ellison. By the time of Brown's death in 1939, Ellison

---

[29]Letter, J. Gratiot to R.S. Ellison, March 23, 1929, private collection. Letter, W.C. Brown to R.S. Ellison, March 31, 1929, private collection.

[30]The sale price was $500. Ellison provided the money to Brown who in turn gave it to Emeline Camp and finally received the long awaited "papers." Letter, W.C. Brown to Mrs. Camp, June 27, 1933, Camp Collection, Custer Battlefield National Monument.

Introduction

had all the Camp papers which Brown had acquired six years before.

Ellison was not as secretive as Camp had been and allowed western scholars to make use of the notes in their research.[31] Among the historians who took advantage of his generosity was Dr. Charles Kuhlman. In the late 1930s, Kuhlman was deep in his research for what was to become his thesis for *Legend into History*. Ellison provided him with extensive excerpts from the Camp material which Kuhlman blended into his masterful reconstruction of the Custer fight. In fact, Kuhlman credited the Camp notes with giving him the basis upon which he built his theory.[32] Ellison continued to work with the Camp notes until his death on August 16, 1945.

Shortly after his passing, Mrs. Ellison presented a large part of her husband's personal papers and extensive library to his alma mater, Indiana University.[33] Included in the papers were some of the Camp notes. In 1967, Mrs. Ellison, in her will, again granted the Lilly Library a large part of the Camp notes. Another segment was acquired by Brigham Young University the following year. It was primarily from this segment that Dr. Hammer chose the interviews and notes for his *Custer in '76*. In addition, a much smaller segment was placed in the Denver Public Library along with some of Ellison's personal papers. Yet, another even smaller fraction was donated to the Custer Battlefield National Monument in 1986. The Camp notes in this book were found in a private collection; the interviews

---
[31]Hammer, "Custer's Man Camp," p. 116.
[32]Charles Kuhlman, *Custer and the Gall Saga* (Billings: n.p., 1940), pp. 3-5.
[33]Hammer, "Custer's Man Camp," p. 117.

and notes for chapters 2, 3, 4 and 6 were placed in the Western History Department of the Denver Public Library following their transcription. Chapters 1, 5 and 7 remain in a private collection.

Students of Western Americana owe to Walter Camp a debt of gratitude which can never be repaid. For years, without any thought of gain or fame, Walter Camp roamed the back roads of the West in search of every Indian War participant he could locate, literally spending days with them while he recorded their stories. Camp was the oral historian par excellence before there was such a title. This debt also extends to General William Brown, who realized just what Camp had accomplished and wanted it preserved for the future. Likewise to Robert Ellison, who had the foresight to ask for Brown's assistance, and for the countless hours he spent in arranging and caring for the papers. Without men such as these whose foresight far exceeded that of their contemporaries, our knowledge of the Indian Wars would indeed be sadly deficient.

CAMP ON CUSTER

Chapter 1

Interviews with John Henley

John Henley (his last name is spelled Hindley on the muster rolls) was born on February 26, 1850, in Philadelphia, Pennsylvania. As a young man, he and his family moved to Indianapolis, Indiana, and at the age of fourteen, Henley enlisted on October 11th as a private in Company "F", 43rd Indiana Volunteer Infantry. He lied on his enlistment papers, telling the recruiter he was eighteen years of age. The following personal information was recorded: five feet one inch in height; dark complexion, eyes and hair; previous occupation, baker. On June 14, 1865, Henley was discharged and fifteen days later he enlisted in Company "A", 13th Infantry (which was reorganized in 1867 and became the 22nd Infantry). His enlistment papers showed him to have grey eyes and was now two and one-half inches taller than in 1864.

Not only was Henley a good soldier, but he was also a healthy one. He was never on sick call during his enlistment. On June 29, 1868, he was discharged at Fort Randall, Dakota Territory, upon expiration of service, as a private. Following his discharge, he worked as a carpenter. However, the military appealed to him and on July 20, 1870, he again enlisted, this time in the 7th Cavalry, and was assigned to "B" Troop. According to the records, he had now reached his adult height of five feet eight and three-quarters inches and that he was twenty-two years old. Henley must have liked the mounted arm of the service, as he advanced to the rank of sergeant before his discharge at Shreveport, Louisiana, on July 20, 1875.

As related to Walter Camp, he stayed in the Shreveport area as a post trader until June 1, 1876, as it was on this day he married

31

Camp on Custer

John Henley, former 1st Sergeant, Company B
Courtesy, Little Bighorn Battlefield National Monument

Nancy Henderson and together they returned to his family's home in Indianapolis. He and his wife then travelled west to Standing Rock Agency, Dakota Territory, where he had employment at the post trader's store.

While at the Agency, on April 22, 1878, Henley again enlisted in the 7th Cavalry, "B" Troop, which conveniently was stationed at the Agency. His prior nine years of military service had made him an experienced veteran and when discharged on April 21, 1883, from what was to be his final enlistment, he was the Troop's first Sergeant. Under the character section at the bottom of the discharge was written: "excellent—a highly cultivated soldier—one that all officers respect and honor." This tribute apparently did not apply to his marriage, as about a month (March 3, 1883) prior to his dis-

Henley Interviews: Introduction

charge, Nancy Henley divorced her husband at Bismarck, North Dakota.

Following his separation from the 7th, Henley returned to Indiana and worked as a merchant. On January 15, 1888, he married Jeannette Laura Schulze (born 1869) at Richmond, Indiana. This marriage, like his first, produced no children, and by 1909 the couple had resided in Oak Park, Illinois, for a number of years.

Henley was now disabled and unable to perform any manual labor. He applied for a Civil War pension. The application stated he had "rheumatism, piles, and varicois veins and heart trouble." He was granted an invalid pension in November at the rate of $10 per month. On September 18, 1910, John Henley suffered a fatal stroke while at home at 1015 Wesley Avenue and was buried two days later in Forest Home Cemetery. His wife lived another twenty-three years and died on April 3rd, never remarrying.

As noted, there are some discrepancies between the information Henley related to Walter Camp and what is recorded on the regimental and pension records in the National Archives. The most conspicuous one appears to be the spelling of his name. However, when one takes into account his illegal underage enlistments, the differences become understandable. Nevertheless, John Henley, no matter how old or how his name was spelled, served his country faithfully and well during his four enlistments.

Camp on Custer

Interview with John Henley

"I was discharged on July 20, 1875, at Shreveport and went into post tradership with Criswell.[34] Soon after this, Benjamin Criswell thought there was not enough money in it for two and I bought him out. Criswell had been discharged 15 days after me and he went home to Virginia and soon came back to re-enlist in his company. We had B and G Companies of 7th Cavalry and I Company of 2nd Infantry (at Shreveport, La.).

"When B & G left for the Little Big Horn expedition in spring of 1876, the business did not pay and I gave it up and went to Indianapolis June 2 or 3, 1876."

Henley was in the War of Rebellion with the 43rd Indiana and was a regular in 13th Infantry. He was in B troop, 7th Cavalry as 1st Sergeant from 1870 to 75 and again from 78-1883.[35] He often befriended Sitting Bull by letting him have more than the regulation 50 rounds to go hunting with.

Henley says Custer was generally regarded as very tyrannical and reckless in fighting.

---

[34] Benjamin Criswell, Sergeant B Company, fought under Reno in both the valley and hilltop fights. He was wounded in the neck in the hilltop fight on June 25. Born in Marshall County, W. Va. Second enlistment Feb. 23, 1876, in Shreveport, La. by Lt. Ben. Hodgson. Discharged April 3, 1877, at Standing Rock, Dakota, as Sergeant of excellent character. He was awarded the Medal of Honor for recovering the body of Lt. Hodgson, bringing up ammunition and encouraging the men in the most exposed conditions under heavy fire. He had hazel eyes, black hair, dark complexion and was 5' 6¼" in height. Kenneth Hammer, *Biographies of the 7th Cavalry* (Ft. Collins: Old Army Press, 1972), pp. 60-61.

[35] This was not the first time Camp had talked with John Henley. Henley had previously given Camp an account of the water party at the Little Bighorn. See Chapter 3 herein, Miscellaneous Notes, page 109-110, and Kenneth Hammer, *Custer in '76* (Provo: Brigham Young Press, 1975), p. 7.

Henley Interviews

Sergeant Benjamin C. Criswell,
Company B
*Courtesy, Little Bighorn
Battlefield National Monument*

Henley says Benteen never liked Custer and had no more to say to him than was absolutely necessary.[36]

Henley says the reason Custer was not scalped or mutilated was that he just happened to be one of those which the Indians did not chance to run upon.[37] He says that Bailey was with burial party and Bailey said there were many others who were neither scalped or mutilated.[38] Some who were not scalped had merely been struck in the head with some instrument like a hatchet.

---

[36] Benteen reiterates much the same in a letter to Goldin. John M. Carroll, *The Benteen-Goldin Letters on Custer and His Last Battle* (N.Y: Liveright, 1974), p. 199. Also see Tal Luther "Benteen, Reno and Custer," *Trail Guide*, (Kansas City Westerners) March 1960, Vol. 5, #1.

[37] Referring to all the citations in Hardorff's book, it becomes clear there were few who were buried in this condition. Richard G. Hardorff, *The Custer Battle Casualties* (El Segundo, CA: Upton and Sons, 1989). In particular, see Douglas D. Scott, et al., *Archaeological Perspectives on the Battle of the Little Big Horn* (Norman: University of Oklahoma Press, 1989), pp. 85-86.

[38] This was John E. Bailey, Private, B Company. Camp also interviewed Bailey, his story can be found on pages 81-84.

Camp on Custer

Regarding the Washita Battle

Henley says Custer was piloted part way to Black Kettle's Cheyennes by the renowned frontiersman, James Bridger.[39] He says Bridger went reluctantly as he had been friends with the Indians and did not desire them to know that he was assisting their enemies. However, after much solicitation, Bridger consented to accompany this command part way and then return. He went within two hours march of the village, told the scouts where they would find it and then turned back.[40]

Henley says the result of this battle has been much overdrawn in popular estimations. He says the main force of Indians was not struck at all, and perhaps it was a good thing for Custer and his men that he did not find them.[41] The number of Indians killed was not large (103).[42] Henley says Custer's orders to have the

---

[39]Henley by his own admission did not join the 7th Cavalry until 1870. Thus he had no personal knowledge of events before this date. Custer was not "piloted" to the Washita by Jim Bridger. Bridger, age 64, was in St. Louis and going blind at this time in his life. Perhaps Henley in his aged condition had confused Bridger with another famous scout, California Joe, who is known to have accompanied Custer.

When Bridger heard that Sheridan was planning a winter campaign on the plains, he traveled to Ft. Hays to urge Sheridan to forget the idea, telling the General: "You can't hunt Indians on the plains in winter, for blizzards don't respect man or beast." Carl C. Rister, *Border Command* (Norman: University of Oklahoma Press, 1944), p. 92.

[40]Custer's scouts on this campaign were Ben Clark, Jack Corbin, Romero, California Joe, and about a dozen Osage Indians. Stan Hoig, *The Battle of the Washita* (Lincoln: University of Nebraska Press, 1976), p. 77.

[41]Custer had struck one of the series of villages stretched out along the Washita River. Without a doubt, the 7th was badly outnumbered if the other villages' warriors were taken into consideration. Charles Brill, *Conquest of the Southern Plains* (Oklahoma City: Golden Saga Pub., 1938), pp. 172-173.

[42]For a good discussion of the number of Indians killed at the Washita, see Stan Hoig, *The Battle of the Washita*, App. C.

band play "Garry Owen" when about to charge was ever a subject of ridicule in the regiment. A sort of joke of long standing. For instance, new recruits would occasionally ask the veterans of the regiment to give reminiscences of this fight when some old trooper or non-commissioned officer would show up. "You wish to hear about the battle of the Washita, do you? Well, Sir, it was 4 o'clock in the morning and the band played 'Garry Owen' " and the whole circle of old vets would begin to laugh. It was seldom that an old member of the regiment would begin this narrative in a serious vein, it being generally considered that the music so often referred to in connection with this battle was entirely out of place.[43]

The 1873 Yellowstone Expedition

We rendezvoused at Yankton in April. All the companies were there except I and D, which were with Reno on the boundary survey.[44]

On the 14th of April there was a big snow storm. The Regiment was at Yankton. It snowed for 3 days

---

[43]As the battle began, Custer had the band play "Garry Owen." It is questionable how many of the troopers heard it, as only one strain was played before the breath moisture had frozen the instruments. Hoig, *The Battle of the Washita*, p. 128. Most accounts of the battle take no exception to the band playing the regimental air. For Custer's own account of the opening of the battle with "Garry Owen," see George A. Custer, *My Life on the Plains* (Lincoln: University of Nebraska Press, n.d.), pp. 334-35.

[44]The troops arrived in Yankton, SD, on April 10, 1873. Roger Darling, *Custer's Seventh Cavalry Comes to Dakota* (El Segundo, Upton & Sons, 1988), p. 52. For an account of the boundary survey Henley spoke about, see John E. Parsons, *West on the 49th Parallel* (NY: William Morrow & Co., 1963).

Camp on Custer

and drove us out of our camp into Yankton. The men took their horses into the city and into freight houses. The snow was up to the top of an 'A' tent.[45] I was Quartermaster Sergeant of B Company then. We waited at Yankton for grass to start and left there May 10 and went up on the east side of the river to Fort Rice where we crossed by boat. Mrs. Custer, Mrs. Calhoun and Mrs. Smith were on this march. They would ride their horses a little each morning and then would go into the ambulance and go to sleep.[46] The boat accompanied us and we took horse feed and other supplies from it occasionally. There were ten companies of the 7th Cavalry, 22nd Infantry and other infantry, but no other cavalry. We had 334 6-mule teams.[47]

We left Ft. Rice after the 1st of June and the command struck west. A detachment of our cavalry went up to Fort Lincoln to escort the surveyors out. The object of our expedition was to guard the surveyors of the Northern Pacific Railroad in their reconnaissance. Gen. Rosseau, Chief Engineer of the Railroad was along with Custer.[48]

We started out and crossed the Heart River and fol-

---

[45] The best account of this blizzard is in Darling's *Custer's Seventh Cavalry Comes to Dakota*. In particular see pages 67-75, the storm actually started on April 13th. For Mrs. Custer's account of this period see Elizabeth B. Custer, *Boots and Saddles* (Norman: University of Oklahoma Press, 1966), pp. 9-20.

[46] The 7th departed Yankton on May 7, for Ft. Rice. Mrs. Custer devoted an entire chapter in *Boots and Saddles* describing their movement to Fort Rice, pp. 26-35. It is a similar account to the one related here by Henley.

[47] According to Alan Rolston, the expedition consisted of elements of the 6th, 8th, 9th, 17th and 22nd Infantry regiments, 10 companies of the 7th Cavalry, and 353 civilians. It had 275 wagons, 2,321 mules and horses, and 600 head of cattle. "The Yellowstone Expedition of 1873," *Montana*, April 1970, Vol. 20, #2. pp. 23-24.

[48] The expedition left Fort Rice on June 20. This was General Thomas Rosser (1836-1910). He served in the Confederate Cavalry and many times engaged his West Point friend, Custer, in severe fighting throughout the Shenandoah Valley. For a full length biography of this former rebel, see Millard and Dean Bushong, *Fightin' Tom Rosser, C.S.A.* (Shippensburg, PA: Beidel Printing House, 1983).

lowed it and when two days out, the surveyors and the detachment of the 7th Cavalry with them overtook us. (Here Custer and Stanley had a tilt. Custer was marching too fast for the infantry to keep up.) Stanley at first cautioned him not to march so fast. Custer apparently did not obey and Stanley finally had to order him to halt.[49]

We crossed the Little Missouri 6 or 8 miles south of where Medora is now and went up a dry creek to get out of the valley of the Little Missouri. Where Belfield is now is where we struck the Badlands. At Fort Sully, 25 miles above Pierre, Custer was boasting of what he could do with the 7th Cavalry.[50] Stanley listened awhile and then said, "General Custer, have you ever met the Sioux? Custer said "No." General Stanley said, "Well General, wait until you have met them before talking too much."

Before we got to Glendive, Stanley found out that Custer had taken a stove along in a wagon in disobedience of orders and Stanley had it broken up and put Custer under arrest. Custer had to march with the officers of the rear guard for several days. This made our brave commander crestfallen.[51] When we got to where Glendive now is, we built a stockade. Then we

---

[49] According to Stanley in a letter to his wife, dated June 28, "I had no trouble with Custer." *Personal Memoirs of Major General David S. Stanley* (Gaithersburg, MD: Olde Soldiers Books, 1987), p. 239. The expedition did not cross the Little Missouri until July 11th.

[50] The original Fort Sully was located on the left bank of the Missouri River about six miles below Ft. Pierre, S.D. It was relocated in 1886 to about 28 miles above Pierre. This second Fort Sully was abandoned in October 1894. Robert W. Frazier, *Forts of the West* (Norman, Univ. of Oklahoma, 1992), pp. 137-138.

[51] According to Capt. Frederick W. Benteen, it was a dispute over a government horse loaned to a civilian (on Rosser's staff) which led to Stanley ordering Custer's arrest. John M. Carroll, *Letters on Custer and His Last Battle* (NY: Liveright, 1974), p. 240. This incident occurred on July 8. In fact Stanley had given permission for Custer to take the stove along while at Fort Rice. Lawrence A. Frost, *Arrest General Custer* (Monroe, MI: Garry Owen Pub., 1987), p. 12. The stove in question was not broken up but abandoned by Custer. According to Calhoun, Custer marched at the rear of the column in "good humor." Ibid., p. 13

Camp on Custer

met the boat and the boat crossed us over to the west side. We had not seen any Indians up to this time. Here we left our "sick, lame and lazy" (Beware of Mrs. Custer's book on this campaign, she has the soldiers fighting all the way out and back).[52]

We left Glendive (perhaps) latter part of July.[53] Some days after leaving Glendive we had notice from Stanley that we were in the Indian country and that there should be no stragglers—the men should keep close to the wagons. I was with the wagon train. About two days after this we had a brush with Indians.

On this day (August 4th), four of us were playing cards in the shade of the wagons, Joe Bernard, Honsinger, Baliran and myself. And I made the remark that I wanted a drink of water badly enough to give $5 for it.[54] We started in the direction of the river but could not see it, and after going 100 yards or so I remarked that we had better not get too far from the wagons.

We were opposite the mouth of the Tongue and five or six miles back from the river. Custer was fighting Indians down in the bottom three miles away. Custer had been blazing the trail and where the going was bad he had been leaving signals in the form of sticks, stones, etc. warning us not to go in certain directions. We went to the left, down a little coulee and here we saw Lt. Hodgson in a rise with the outer guard. We found some tepid rain water in a little hollow and took

---

[52] If one reads Chapter 8 devoted to the Yellowstone Expedition pages, 68-74 of Mrs. Custer's *Boots and Saddles* there is no impression conveyed that the soldiers were fighting all the time.

[53] The command arrived at the Yellowstone River about 8 miles above the mouth of Glendive Creek. Here a cantonment was constructed, named Camp Thorne. The expedition arrived there on July 12 and left on July 26. Rolston, "The Yellowstone Expedition," p. 26.

[54] According to Lt. Charles Larned, Honsinger and Baliran were after water for their horses and not for themselves. George F. Howe "Expedition to the Yellowstone River in 1873," *The Mississippi Valley Historical Review*, Dec. 1952, Vol. 39, #3, p. 532.

Henley Interviews: Yellowstone Expedition

a drink, but it was very warm. Honsinger and Baliran (mounted) had gone straight ahead on the trail of Custer about ½ or ¾ mile ahead of me. Honsinger had a heavy horse and Baliran a mustang pony (Baliran was the Sutler of 7th Cavalry. Honsinger was Chief Veterinary of 7th Cavalry). Not over 20 minutes after Honsinger and Baliran (Baliran had a small pocket pistol) had left us, we came up to them with the train and saw a commotion ahead. When we found Baliran, with three arrows in him and a bullet hole clear through, he was just gasping his last. One foot was doubled up under him and when I pulled his coat open powder smoke came out. I think the Indian had pushed his gun against Baliran's body and fired and the smoke lodged inside his garments. The three arrows were in his back and one had missed the ribs and gone clear through. General Custer's Striker saw this and said there was no use of leaving the arrow sticking in his body and so pulled it on through (in the direction it had entered). Baliran lay in the bottom and Honsinger was on the side hill 100 yards away. I think his horse had started up the bank, but the Indians had caught him. He was hit with an arrow in the kidneys and bruised on the forehead. No bullet was in him. He was dead when found. Both horses had been taken along by Indians, but we found Honsinger's horse 48 hours ahead on our march, shot dead. The horse was hard to manage and the Indians probably could not get along with him.[55]

---

[55] This is substantially the same account as given by Louis Hill. However, Bugler Hill stated he witnessed the killings and both Honsinger and Baliran were on foot when the Indians killed them. In fact he confirms the bruise on Honsinger's forehead, as Hill said "a big Indian rode up and struck him (Honsinger) over the head with the stock of his gun." Louis Hill, "With General Custer in the Northern Pacific Surveying Expedition of 1873," *By Valor and Arms*, Oct. 1974, Vol. 1, #1, p. 52. This occurred on August 4.

Camp on Custer

Those Indians had slipped in between Custer (who was fighting down in the bottom) and the train and killed Honsinger and Baliran.

Honsinger was brought back to where Baliran was—slung across a horse—and when the ambulance came along they were loaded in and taken down to the camp where Custer had been fighting (close to the river Custer's skirmish line had rested right on the river), down in the bottom and buried them between 2 good sized trees. There were scattered cottonwood trees around. They were killed 3 miles from the river and were buried within a ¼ mile of the river or closer.

First we put down a matting of shrubbery and wrapped the men in blankets. Then we put on brush and stone (to keep wolves from digging them up) and dirt on top and stamped it down hard and then trod horses over them so that we might obliterate all traces of a grave.

This same day, one of our soldiers had been killed, off to the right, and we did not find him until our return on the campaign. The curious thing about it was that his gun was with him. His horse was gone. He must have been wounded and got away from the Indians and then died.[56]

When Custer was on the skirmish line the Indians fought in a half circle and there was a medicine man displaying himself, showing his bravery. Bloody Knife asked permission to go out and get him and at first Custer would not consent, but finally Custer said, "Go,

---

[56] This trooper was Private John H. Ball of F Company 7th Cavalry, Dr. Lawrence A. Frost, *Custer's 7th Cav and the Campaign of 1873* (El Segundo: Upton & Sons, 1986), p. 69. Later on the expedition as Henley relates, they found out what happened to Ball—Custer's Scouts reported: "He had fired one shot and then had been killed. They (the Sioux) captured his horse, saddle and equipage." *N.Y. Times*, Sept. 9, 1873.

but be careful." Bloody Knife rode out 500 yards and when within 300 yards of the Medicine Man he fired and shot him through the breast.[57] The Indians rode up promptly and carried the dead Medicine Man off between them. The next day we found the Medicine Man's clothing hidden in some brush and the bullet hole was through his shirt, which was soaked with blood.

We made one or two days march and that night Custer got permission to pull out with 5 days rations and 8 companies.[58] We took the trail that night and followed it all night until 5 a.m. and had orders to make coffee with dry twigs so as not to make smoke. We stopped for 1 hour and at 6 a.m. went on until noon when the horses began to wear out, having made about 80 miles since the morning of the day before.

We rested until 2 or 3 o'clock and went on until we found the trail went right into the river. We supposed they had crossed and thought we could follow them no further, but afterwards found it was a blind trail. They had gone over across a sand bar in the direction of the other shore, but had cut across a bend and came back on the same side, as we found out the next day. We lay here all day, the officers debating what they should do. Here Custer decided he would swim the river by companies with 3 days rations and 100 rounds of ammunition. Charlie Reynolds advised against it and told Custer if he would lie here 48 hours he could have all

---

[57]In Custer's report of this fight he wrote: "The first Indian killed was shot from his pony by Bloody Knife." Custer, *Boots and Saddles*, p. 239. This is the only detailed account of the circumstances which led to this Indian's death.

[58]On August 8th the scouts discovered a fresh Sioux trail and Stanley ordered Custer to take the cavalry and pursue the Indians to their village. Rolston, "The Yellowstone Expedition," p. 27.

Camp on Custer

the fight he wanted.[59] Never the less, to satisfy Custer, Reynolds had his partner and scout (whose full name I can't recall, but it was Bill) swim the river with his horse. This he did by stripping himself. He carried just a belt and a knife and only a surcingle on his horse (no saddle).[60] He swam across to other shore and went into the brush and timber and remained over there about 30 minutes. He then walked his horse up along shore and started back. He kept his horse's head turned quarter-wise up stream—with one hand on the bridle and the other on the surcingle while floating. I thought I would go down to hear what he had to say when landing.

When he struck shore, Charlie Reynolds grabbed his hand and asked him what he found over there. Both he and his horse were badly out of breath, but he gasped out, "Why the woods over there are full of them. I saw them all around me. I only waited to catch my breath before I started back. I did not feel safe until I got half way back." Charlie said, "Are you sure?" He replied "Sure? Why I saw a great many of them."[61]

Soon after this Custer came up to talk with Reynolds and the Scout. Custer heard that the Indians were over there and asked if he thought the Indians would wait for him to go over (Custer was still deter-

---

[59] Not all the scouts counseled patience. Bloody Knife begged Custer to attack at once and when they did not, said the "whites harbored little bird hearts, that they were afraid to fight the Dakotas." Ben Innis, *Bloody Knife* (Ft. Collins, CO: Old Army Press, 1973), p. 89.

[60] This could have been Billy Jackson. However, he makes no mention of this event in his book. James Willard Schultz, *William Jackson, Indian Scout* (Boston: Houghton Mifflin & Co. 1926) p. 107-110. A surcingle is a strap passed around a horse's body to bind on a saddle.

[61] It is hard to judge this conversation. The scout could have done what was reported. However, Lt. James Calhoun recorded: "One of our Indian scouts who was directed to ascertain how deep the water was found he could wade to a small island about midway between the two banks. As nothing could be done that night, we went into camp" Dr. Lawrence A. Frost, *Some Observations on the Yellowstone Expedition, 1873* (Glendale: Arthur H. Clark Co. 1980), p. 72.

mined to go over) and fight them. There it was that he said if Custer would wait 48 hours the Indians would come over and give him all the fight he wanted. (We had followed a blind trail to this point. A mile above and below the Indians had crossed, but with little swimming where the current widened out). Custer had at first proposed to swim.

Two or three herders had followed our trail all night long and caught up with us with some badly played out steers. Some of these were ordered killed and the meat was issued to the troops and the hides were stretched in the sun flat out to dry for the bull boats.[62]

Bloody Knife and the scouts made a frame of saplings and the next morning stretched the hide over it and made the boat. This was a detail under Weston, etc. A rope made of tying lariats together was stretched to a sand bar by pulling it out along shore and a man swimming over on a log. When he landed on the bar and tried to fasten it, the force of the current snapped it.

It had been intended to use the bull boat to carry over supplies and men and to swim the horses.

After the rope snapped, Custer gave up this scheme and intended the next day to swim by companies. I was in the fifth company from the front and we laughed about it, well knowing the first company that tried it would fail and come back and we would never have to try it.[63]

The Indians saved us that trouble, for before day-

[62]The idea to use bull boats to move the command across the river came from Charlie Reynolds and Gilman Norris. They suggested Bloody Knife and the Arikaras build them. Frost, *Custer's 7th Cav*, p. 81.

[63]The reason why the army was having such a problem on crossing the Yellowstone, while the Indians were able to transverse it at will, was explained by Basil Clement: "The river was very deep and swift, and our American horses would not take it." Charles E. DeLand, "Basil Clement," *South Dakota Historical Collections*, 1922, Vol. 11, p. 372.

light the next morning they were over on our side, having swam the river both above us and below us. The fight was started by a shot across the river to attract our attention. I picked up my gun and ran to the bank to get a view of where the firing was and just as I exposed myself, I saw the bullets cutting the grass around me. Lt. Hodgson, who was behind a tree, cried out: "Sergeant Henley, get back, get back. Don't you see they are firing at you. Get back." Just at this time Criswell, my bunkie, was leading a cream-colored horse. It was struck below the eye and killed dead. This horse was the first thing struck. In the fighting across the river, Custer's favorite Orderly, Tuttle, was killed[64] and one in the band was struck in the haversack and jarred a little but not hurt. Another one of my company who went to the river with canteens for water was wounded in the fleshy part of his arm (Henley says that the leader in getting water was a man named Collins of either B or D troop, who first made a dash and got back all right and that encouraged others).[65] After the firing started, Custer had the band strike up Garry Owen, but the noise of the firing drowned out the music and it sounded ridiculous enough, etc.[66]

---

[64]This was Private John H. Tuttle, Company E. "When the firing commenced in the morning, he (Tuttle) took a Springfield sporting rifle and with two other men, took station behind a tree and began picking off the Indians as they exposed themselves on the opposite bank. He had killed three Indians in the following manner: Observing one in full view on the bank, he remarked to the men with him, "watch me drop that buck," fired and down the Indian went, two others rushed to the assistance of the one killed, and Tuttle by rapid use of his breech loader, succeeded in killing them both. The Indians naturally became enraged at this kind of slaughter and directed their fire at Tuttle who incautiously looking out to get another shot, received a ball over his left eye which killed him instantly." Frost, *Some Observations*, pp. 74-75.

[65]This was Private John C. Collins of Company G.

[66]In Custer's report of this fight, he made mention of having the band immediately in

Henley Interviews: Yellowstone Expedition

The Indians had now got in below us on our side and were firing on Capt. French's Company, which was the company farthest down that way (This fight was opposite the mouth of the Big Horn). We were now ordered back from the river up a coulee. We had stood there mounted for about 10 minutes when Lt. Ketcham's horse was killed (Ketcham was acting Adjutant General of the whole expedition under Stanley.[67] We had 17 companies of infantry on this expedition and six pieces of artillery.[68] One 6 lb. "long tom" Parrott and the rest brass pieces). About the same time, Custer's horse was shot in the shoulder and was bleeding badly and Custer came riding back. Ketcham said, "General my horse is shot." Custer said excitedly "So is mine, give me a horse, any horse, Dandy, the sorrel." He then said to 1st Lt. Tom Custer, who was commanding my company, "Charge them, Tom. Damn them. Charge them." We then charged right up the coulee and were right upon them.[69] I said to Tom Custer: "There is an Indian, there is one," referring to a dismounted one and he replied: "Never mind the one, go for the bunch." We took for the bunch and I followed one and took five shots at him just ahead of

---

the rear of the skirmish line play "Garry Owen" as the squadrons took to the gallop after the Indians. Frost, *Some Observations*, p. 129.

[67] Hiram H. Ketchum. Born Canada. Private Company K, 16th N.Y. Vol. 20 Sept. 1861. Discharged 24 Sept. 1862. Private Company I, 1st N.Y. Eng. 10 Sept. 1864. Discharged 30 May 1865. 2nd Lt. 13th Infantry 23 Feb. 1866. Transferred to 22nd Infantry 21 Sept. 1866, 1st Lt. 31 July 1867. Regimental Adjutant 1 March 1869 to 1 Oct. 1881. Captain 20 July 1882, Major 26 April 1898. Died 12 Aug. 1898. Col. Powell, *List of Officers*, p. 412.

[68] According to Stanley's report, there were two artillery squads formed, servicing the artillery's only two 3 inch Rodman guns. Frost, *Some Observations*, p. 87. There were 18 companies of infantry, 5 from the 8th, 6 from the 9th, 3 from the 17th and 5 from the 22nd Infantry.

[69] Tom Custer and B Company charged the Indians on the right of the line. He was supported by Captain Yates and Moylan. Frost, *Custer's 7th Cav*, p. 84.

Camp on Custer

me. My first shot struck under his horse's heels as I saw it hit the dust, but of the remaining four, I heard every one hit him, but he kept in the saddle and looked around wildly. I thought he would turn to the right, but he fooled me and turned suddenly to the left and I went off to the right. There he got away from me. We followed them for about 3¼ miles and stopped and thought we were alone. Here we dismounted and commenced firing as skirmishers.[70] A soldier named Guthrie slipped up behind me and fired off his carbine close to my ear and I thought sure I was hit in the head.[71] I was stunned momentarily and found myself feeling my head to see where I was hit. We were firing here 15 or 30 minutes and I fired 20 rounds at this dismount. We were now ordered to mount up and charge further.

After I mounted up my horse, 'Zachariah' took the bit in his teeth and ran away with me, going straight for the Indians. I got so close to them that I, in desperation, wound the bridle in one hand as far ahead as I could reach and pulled with all my might and pulled his head around to the left and got him turned. The Indians were riding toward us in a half moon and one Indian made to cut me off. He got closer than I ever wanted an Indian to get again and fired. But he was more excited than I was, for when he fired his gun, it was pointed up in the air. I was close enough to him to see that he wore a rim of a hat with the crown gone and a feather sticking in it between the rim and his

---

[70]"As the four companies charged, the Indians stopped, dismounted and fired, then mounted and retreated a short distance. Then dismounted again while the soldiers would ride up near them, then they would dismount and fire a volley into the Indians." Hill, "With General Custer...," p. 54.

[71]This was Private George Guthrie, B Company.

Henley Interviews: Yellowstone Expedition

head. By this time I was cutting a circle back and saw the Company coming up. When they got up, I was dismounted, kicking the horse. I had pulled so hard on the bit that I had his mouth bleeding badly and my boots were all splattered with blood. When the Company got up, Tom Custer yelled: "Here now, that is enough of that. Mount up and fall in." We only went a short distance when the Indians veered off to the left and toward the river and we stopped on a brow of a hill and saw some mounted men off to the right in the distance. At first we took them for Indians, but when they made a maneuver, we could see the guidons against the sky and knew they were our men.

Sometime during the fight, off to our right, Lt. Braden was hit. He was carried a long distance in a blanket.[72] Tuttle, Custer's orderly had been killed behind a tree down at the river before we left it, in the beginning of the fight.[73]

The fight was now over, for the Indians had disappeared and we went back to the river. When we had been fighting on the skirmish line we had heard the booming of artillery and it was still firing when we got back to the river. After sundown, we first thought it was thunder, but the regularity of the intervals between the sound told us it was artillery firing. Stanley was firing at the Indians across the river with his ar-

---

[72]Charles Braden. Born Michigan. USMA 1865-1869. 2nd Lt. U.S. 7th Cavalry, 30 June 1869. 1st Lt. 9 Dec. 1875. Retired 28 June, 1878. Brevet 1st Lt. 28, Feb. 1890 for gallant service against Indians in Big Horn, Montana, 11 Aug. 1873 when he was severely wounded. Powell, *List of Officers*, p. 205. For Braden's personal account of the fight, his wound and the long arduous journey back to civilization, see Charles Braden, "An Incident of the Yellowstone Expedition of 1873," *Cavalry Journal*, Oct. 1904, Vol. 15, #54, pp. 289-301.

[73]"General Custer ordered Tuttle's body to be sewed up in canvas and placed in an ambulance, for he thought a great deal of him, and we buried him the next night at sundown in a cottonwood grove near the river." Hill, "With General Custer...," p. 55.

Camp on Custer

tillery, having heard our firing, and hurried forward. Every man now yelled: "Stanley is up, Stanley is up."[74] On our way down to camp after fighting all day, we stopped to see the fireworks of Stanley shelling the Indians across the river. It was one of the prettiest sights I ever saw. The Indians on our side of the river had now given up the fight and crossed back again both above us and below us and Stanley shelled them across the river until they disappeared.[75] Tuttle was the only man killed out right in the day's fight.[76]

The evening of this day I saw three officers sitting on a log talking. One of these was Capt. Yates. I heard one of them make the remark: "Gentlemen, it is only a question of time until Custer will get us into a hole from which we will not escape."

After reflection, Henley thinks this fight was opposite the mouth of the Big Horn.

We buried Tuttle that night and pulled out the next morning and went to Pompey's Pillar and laid there 3 days. The middle of the next forenoon about 200 men were bathing in the river and a few Indians came up on the opposite bank and fired two shots.[77] There was great excitement and scrambling and all ran hurriedly out, crying: "Johnny get your gun." There was no more

---

[74]Stanley had heard the firing about 8 A.M. on that day (August 11) and ordered his artillery forward to support the cavalry. They made a mad dash, set up, and began shelling the woods on the opposite bank where Indians had retreated. Frost, *Custer's 7th Cav*, p. 86.

[75]Basil Clement claimed he directed the artillery "to shell these groups,...several shells well aimed produced a wonderful scampering out of sight. An hour afterwards, a few more shells at a group of warriors caused the fastest kind of running." DeLand, "Basil Clement," p. 372.

[76]"Our loss was one killed, Private Tuttle, E Troop, and 3 wounded. Lt. Charles Braden in the thigh, Pvt. Englebert Taylor in the left arm and Private John in the leg." "Camp on the Musselshell River," *Chicago Interocean*, August 19, 1873.

[77]This incident occurred on August 16th. The command arrived at Pompey's Pillar the day before.

Henley Interviews: Yellowstone Expedition

firing and the excitement died down. About midnight that night, a man on picket saw something moving (perhaps a wolf), and fired at it and alarmed the whole camp. Everybody got up and began some firing, and an uproar followed. Custer was on hand promptly and cried out: "Stop that firing. Don't you know that Indians will not attack in the night." After lying here three days (we went no further), we struck across for the Musselshell. We were now on Baker's trail and when we struck the Musselshell we found a herd of cattle that Baker had left.[78] Stanley ordered them killed and issued to the troops and we had plenty of beef.

We followed the Musselshell east until it turned north, and then we left it and struck off straight east and came to the Yellowstone again, not far from mouth of Powder (On this march, Custer was breaking the trail and one day Stanley asked him if he did not think he was selecting too rough country. Custer said no, and continued. Stanley went off without saying anything.)

That night we found a good spot and made camp. We looked ahead and saw two men riding up. They proved to be a Lieutenant and an Orderly. They came up and reported to Custer that Stanley was in camp 5 miles ahead of him. Stanley had left Custer's trail and taken a ridge and gone around and beaten him.[79] This was a blow to Custer who wanted to pull right out, but

---

[78]The trail Henley refers to was the one made by Major Eugene Baker in 1872. The command had a fight with the Sioux near Billings, Montana, on August 14th. This attack was beaten off and Baker moved to Pompey's Pillar before returning to Fort Ellis. Rolston, "The Yellowstone Expedition of 1873," p. 22.

[79]For a different account of this incident which is the opposite of Henley's, refer to Frost, *Custer's 7th Cav*, p. 98. In it Custer was the one who was ahead of Stanley and had found the best route.

Camp on Custer

Stanley's order was for him to camp where he was until the next day. When this news became noised around the camp, someone said they would wager Custer would move as soon as midnight and he did. We had breakfast about 1 a.m. and before 2 a.m. were on the march to overtake Stanley. The Northern Pacific Railroad engineers were with us all of this time. We proceeded to the stockade (Glendive) and crossed the river to the east side.[80] In an officers' tent there was a wager made by Custer that he would beat Stanley to Ft. Lincoln by 3 days. Custer was to stop with the engineers one day in the Badlands and took the best mules and wagons.[81] The result was that Custer got to Ft. Lincoln late in the evening (after sundown), and Stanley got in at 10 a.m. the next day.[82] Therefore Custer lost his bet. Stanley was considered one of the best topographical engineers in the army and a very good marcher. His reputation for marching infantry was great. Fred Grant was along on this expedition.[83]

On this campaign it had not been Stanley's plan to hunt Indians to fight them, but only to assume the defensive and protect the surveyors.[84] Custer, however, was always eager to fight.

---

[80]They arrived at the stockade on Sept. 9th.

[81]Custer marched for Ft. Lincoln on Sept. 12th. It is hard to say at this late date what kind of wagers, if any, took place. However, Stanley's report stated he dispatched Custer to Ft. Lincoln. Custer was to survey the Badlands on his way there. Stanley, *Personal Memoirs*, pp. 252-54.

[82]Custer's command arrived at Ft. Lincoln on 21st of Sept. Stanley arrived on the 23rd.

[83]Frederick Dent Grant was the son of then President Ulysses S. Grant. Born in Missouri and appointed at large to USMA in 1867. 2nd Lt. 4th Cavalry, 12 June 1871. Lt. Col. Aide-de-Camp to Lt. Gen. 17 March, 1873, 1st Lt. 4th Cav. 28 June 1876. Resigned 1 Oct. 1881. Brig. Gen. U.S. Volunteers 1898. Powell, *List of Officers*, p. 338.

[84]This statement about assuming a defensive position is not in agreement with other accounts. See in particular an article in the *N.Y. Tribune*, June 28, 1873, "Exploration of Central Montana." It claimed Stanley's command would protect the surveyors, intimidate and subdue the Indians, locate potential fort sites and conduct a scientific reconnaissance of the area.

Henley Interviews: Yellowstone Expedition

Stanley was shelling the Indians across the river. The Indians would try to get up the bluff and a shell would strike ahead of them and explode and back to the river they would run. Then they would start up the river and a shell would head them off. It was amusing to see their behavior under shell fire.[85]

In the expedition Custer had a large pack of greyhounds. A Lieutenant in the 22nd Infantry had a dog much swifter and in one chase after an antelope this superiority became easily apparent, not a little to the annoyance of Custer.

Seven or eight days out of the cantonment two of the dogs got footsore and hung behind and instead of following up, took their back track for the cantonment. When they came down over the hill opposite the cantonment and when they got to the river, someone called and one of the dogs swam over, nearly famished. Both dogs were nearly starved. After this dog was fed, he grabbed a mouth full of bones and started to go across the river to feed his partner. When these hounds were seen coming in, there was all sorts of conjecture as to what had happened.

On this expedition Col. Grant, for some reason or other, went back and was not in the battle.[86] On this expedition Calhoun was Adjutant and A. E. Smith Quartermaster.[87]

We met Gen. Stanley at Ft. Sully, 25 miles above Pierre, but he went from there to Ft. Lincoln by boat

---

[85] All accounts agree as to the effect the artillery fire had upon the Indians. See Frost, *Custer's 7th Cav*, p. 86 for one of the best recollections.

[86] Grant left the Stockade at Glendive for Ft. Lincoln upon learning of the death of his grandfather. From Ft. Lincoln he continued on to Chicago. Frost, *Some Observations*, pp. 136-37.

[87] This was Lt. James Calhoun of C Company. The quartermaster was Lt. Algernon E. Smith of A Company.

Camp on Custer

and did not join us until he came out from Lincoln and met us two or three days march out of there.[88]

On this trip, Baliran the sutler, had several barrels of whiskey and it was against orders and he became alarmed and distributed it among the different companies—a barrel to each company.[89] Our company had a barrel of it in its wagon. Adjutant General Ketcham (1st Lt. in 22nd Infantry) went hunting around and discovered it and took an ax and smashed the barrels[90] and spilled it on the ground and some of the men got down on their hands and knees and drank enough of it to get drunk and a hilarious old time resulted.[91]

---

[88]This basically agrees with Stanley's report of the expedition. "Report on the Yellowstone Expedition 1873" by D. S. Stanley, Colonel 22nd Infantry, Bvt. Major General U.S.A., Washington, 1874.

[89]That Stanley had a problem with whiskey is well documented by the participants on the expedition. Carroll, *The Benteen-Goldin Letters*, p. 356. Marguerite Merington, *The Custer Story* (NY: Devin-Adair Co., 1950), p. 251-252, Frost, *Custer's 7th Cav*, p. 176. Stanley had given his permission at Ft. Rice for Baliran to accompany the expedition. He also knew Baliran had whiskey along with his sutler supplies. On June 23rd Stanley ordered Col. Fred Grant to destroy the liquor. Col. Grant told Custer about the order and said to hide the whiskey before he "came to inspect." Merington, *The Custer Story*, p. 252. Before Grant could look for the hidden intoxicants Stanley canceled the order. Ibid., p. 252.

[90]This incident occurred on July 22 according to a *N.Y. Times* report (August 10, 1872). Lt. Ketcham and Ray assisted by the provost guard "seized the stock of the sutler as barrel after barrel was rolled out of the wagon. Lt. Ray, axe in hand, demolished the heads of the barrels, and gallons upon gallons of liquor soon saturated the ground." Benteen, always on the lookout for Benteen, wrote to Goldin that Ketcham and Ray, came at dawn "axes in hand and spilt the good liquor....at the stockade camp. Grant, Gibson, Weston and myself had procured a quart one-half hour before destruction...Stanley was stupidly drunk at the time." Carroll, *The Benteen-Goldin Letters*, p. 256. Ketcham had done this to destroy Stanley's supply and keep the commanding officer sober enough as to not delay the expedition any longer. Maria B. Kimball, *Soldier-Doctor of our Army* (NY: Houghton-Mifflin Co., 1917), p. 29. Custer wrote to his wife about the delays: "Yesterday we marched at noon, but only five miles before going into camp. Everybody is chafing at the delay...whiskey alone is the cause. You have no idea how this has delayed the expedition, and added to the government expense." Merington, *The Custer Story*, p. 260.

[91]The *N.Y. Times* article of August 10th reported the comments of a soldier who watched the whiskey being poured out. "... that it was just the ground where he'd like to be buried." The article further stated the sutler had been selling the product for $12 a gallon.

Henley Interviews: Yellowstone Expedition

Braden was not taken in an ambulance because it jarred him too much, so he was carried a long distance on a stretcher.[92]

Henley said a short time before Baliran (trader) and Honsinger (post veterinary surgeon) were killed, he was playing cards with them and that he and another soldier and Baliran and Honsinger had gone after drinking water and warned them not to go in the direction they did. When they came back they found them shot with bullets and arrows.

Yellowstone Campaign—(Henley says that the part of the fight he was in started about 5 miles east of the mouth of the Big Horn on the north side of the river) We must have gone 4 miles westward in our charges so that the battle ended well toward the mouth of the Big Horn.[93]

On this expedition I saw three officers who were sitting on a log and predicting that Custer would some day get them into a hole from which they could not get out.

The men were congratulating themselves on the fact that they did not cross the river into the ambush of the Indians as Custer was so anxious to do, also on the timely arrival of Stanley. Undoubtedly the withdrawal of the Indians was caused by the approach of Stanley that afternoon.

---

[92] For a drawing of the stretcher used to carry Lt. Braden, see Braden, "An Incident of the Yellowstone Expedition," p. 293.

[93] Dr. Vance Haynes has done considerable work in locating the sites of Custer's Yellowstone Battles. His research was published in "Custer's Yellowstone Battle," *Report on Research Anthropology*, Vol. 7, #2, pp. 16-18.

Camp on Custer

Regarding the Black Hills

Fred Grant had command of one of the wings.[94]

About June 15, 1874, we moved 2 or 3 miles out of the post and camped for two weeks to see what we would need on the campaign. We started out about July 2 toward the hills.[95] The six mule teams were loaded to 5,900 lbs. besides the wagon.

Before starting Custer had guaranteed that the expedition would not have a cost to exceed $500.00, over and above ordinary expense to the regiment. The forage that he would get would offset much of the extra expense. Before we got back, Lt. McIntosh told me the extra expense had already exceeded this by several times.[96] There were many civilians along and by Custer's orders, they were riding cavalry horses. The St. Paul *Pioneer Press* man was along.[97] He started out driving a wagon, but when we got into the hills, he got a horse and the enlisted man who rode the horse was detailed to drive the wagon.[98]

---

[94]Grant was not assigned to command a wing. He was merely an acting aide to Custer. The Battalion (wing) assignment went to Major George A. Forsyth and Major Joseph Tilford. Donald Jackson, *Custer's Gold* (New Haven: Yale University, 1966), p. 20.

[95]The command went into camp on the Little Heart River 2 miles below Ft. Lincoln on June 14. The expedition left for the Black Hills on July 2nd. Dr. Lawrence A. Frost, *With Custer in '74* (Provo: Brigham Young Press, 1974), p. 1.

[96]Henley's statement that the expedition cost the government money is at variance with others recorded. Custer was asked to detail his budget in a letter personally addressed to Lt. Gen. Philip Sheridan. In it Custer estimated a savings of at least $19,437 on animal feed alone by foraging the horses along the route. Frost, *With Custer in '74*, p. xvi. *The Chicago Interocean* for Sept. 8, 1874 reported: "Gen. Custer had been mistaken only in the amount of the balance, which was found on the return of the expedition to have been over $16,000." *The New York World* for Sept. 12, 1874 remarked that he (Custer) saved the government between $20,000 and $30,000. Jackson perhaps said it best: "Soldiers had to be fed whether on the march or in quarters. It was cheaper to go than stay." *Custer's Gold*, p. 17.

[97]This was Aris B. Donaldson. Mr. Donaldson also served as the expedition's botanist.

Lt. Col. George A. Custer donning the "long hair" which became a legend among the Indians he fought and the soldiers he led. Photo by O.S. Goff, 1873, Ft. Lincoln, D.T.
Courtesy, Paul Harbaugh Collection

The first two days we made an average of 15 miles per day and after this went faster. Horses were on ⅓ rations and grazed out at night, lariated and hobbled.

We struck out southwest and stuck very near the corners of Dakota, Montana and Wyoming. There we buried the two men who had died of dysentery and another fellow who was shot in a quarrel and died.[99] The man who shot him did so in self defense. Custer

---

[98]William E. Curtis, a reporter on the expedition representing *The Chicago Inter-Ocean*, wrote (July 27, 1873) "Mr. Donaldson had his own horse by the name of "Dobbin" who was described as a long, lank beast, very deliberated in his movements, but perfectly docile." Henley could have had this incident confused with some other.

[99]This was Private John Cunningham of H Company who died July 21 of dysentery. Private George Turner was shot and killed July 22 by Private William Roller. Both were of M Company. For a detailed description of the fight and the shooting of Turner, see John M. Carroll and Dr. Lawrence A. Frost, *Private Theodore Ewert's Diary of the Black Hills Expedition of 1874*, (NJ: CRF Books, 1976), pp. 36-38.

made him walk the whole expedition and back to Ft. Lincoln. Here he was tried and acquitted and awarded two years pay and allowances.[100]

We went south from here, east of the Wyoming line through the hills and to Castle Creek,[101] coming down this creek into Indians so suddenly that we captured a number of them.[102] Custer let them all go but one old Indian who he kept to pilot him through the hills.[103] Some of the Indian scouts wanted to scalp him (Lynch says Bloody Knife wanted to). Custer kept the Indian under guard every night to protect him and finally when he got within a day's march of his people, let him go well supplied with provisions and some money.[104]

Here we got into a bad place and had a hard time pulling out of it.[105] We then went down to Custer City

---

[100] Carroll and Frost both claimed Roller was in prison at the time of the Battle of the Little Bighorn for the killing of Turner. Ibid., p. 36. However, Henley is correct. William Roller "was placed under arrest immediately after the shooting and under the order of Gen. Custer and was compelled to walk thenceforth throughout the rest of his expedition until the return to Ft. Lincoln. He was then turned over to the civil authorities on the charge of murder at Yankton, but was eventually turned loose and returned to his command where he served out his enlistment." Jesse Brown and A. M. Willard, *The Black Hills Trails* (NY: Arno Press, 1975), p. 36.

[101] For a good account of the expedition through Wyoming, see Mabel Brown, "The Wyoming Portion of the Custer Expedition of 1874 to Explore the Black Hills" *Annals of Wyoming*, Fall 1974, Vol. 46, #2.

[102] The capture of One Stab and his band of 27 Ogallalas occurred on July 26. Jackson, *Custer's Gold*, p. 77-78.

[103] Henley was correct. Custer needed the Sioux to "pilot" him. "What Custer wanted from these people was information. His maps were no longer adequate and his guides knew almost nothing about the Hills." Ibid., p. 79.

[104] Custer released One Stab on August 5. According to a dispatch by A. B. Donaldson in the *Daily Pioneer* (August 24th) it was not Bloody Knife but the Arikaras Bear's Ears and Mad Bull who wanted to kill and scalp One Stab. However, Ben Innis stated Bloody Knife also wanted to kill the Ogallala and was disgusted when permission was denied. Innis, *Bloody Knife*, pp. 104-105.

[105] July 29 was an extremely difficult day for the command on the march. "The canyon or ravine through which we traveled was narrow, full of rocks, and up by a creek. The rocks had to be removed and the creek bridged every half a mile and once the point of a mountain had to be dug down so wagons could pass." Carroll and Frost, *Private Theodore Ewert's Diary*, p. 48.

and went into camp and remained there 5 or 6 days.¹⁰⁶

At Custer City there was not even a cabin, we had with the expedition an expert miner named McGhee (or McGee).¹⁰⁷ After we had encamped McGhee got down into the creek bed and said there was gold there. There was an expert there from Washington who asked him how he knew. He replied: "I don't know how, but I can show you." So he went to panning and soon had some colors panned out and exhibited it. He panned considerable material, but said the gold was not in sufficient quantity to pay—said a man might make $1.50 per day or $3.00 or perhaps nothing. McGhee and I went hunting together from here.¹⁰⁸

We washed our clothes here and took a good swim every day. and came out of the hills south of Custer City on Box Elder Creek near Rapid City. From here we went up east of Bear Butte.¹⁰⁹

Before we got to Custer City, Custer with one troop and the scouts made a side trip of exploration over toward Whitewood Creek and stayed 4 or 5 days. He had told us to wait for him for 3 days. After he overstayed this time we began to be concerned about him, fearing he had met with misfortune.¹¹⁰ Then, at last, he came marching in. We were much relieved. It ap-

---

[106] The Expedition was camped in the vicinity of the present day Custer, S.D., from July 30 through August 4.

[107] There was no civilian miner by the name of McGhee or McGee on the expedition. Henley could have meant McKay. Horatio Ross and William McKay were the two miners taken along by Custer. Jackson, *Custer's Gold*, p. 144.

[108] On August 1st gold was found. Ross thought the gold at this place would yield $50 or $75 per day. Herbert Krause and Gary Olson, *Prelude to Glory* (Sioux Falls: Brevet Press, 1974), pp. 126-27. Jackson, *Custer's Gold*, pp. 84-85.

[109] For Custer's route leaving the Black Hills see Donald R. Progulske, *Following Custer* (Brookings: South Dakota State University, n.d.).

[110] The incident Henley describes here is the same one related by Lt. Calhoun. On August 3, Custer with 5 companies and the engineers left on a side trip to explore the south fork of the Cheyenne River. Frost, *With Custer in '74*, pp. 61-69.

Camp on Custer

peared that his delay had been caused by getting lost. He had with him on this trip, however, the old Indian for a guide.

Charlie Reynolds was sent to Laramie to carry Custer's report of what he had found and he also carried news of the discovery of gold and took some of the color with him.[111] In starting he was escorted by some officers and a troop, and they left him at dusk. He had boots for his horse and traveled only at night at first, but got within 3 days of Laramie and made big time. He went well supplied with field glasses and compass. Once on the trip he spied Indians, but avoided them and after this saw no more of them.[112]

Sgt. Criswell and I were bunkies on this trip and we had been preserving our rations in anticipation of a shortage. It happened that 3 days before got back we ran short of rations and men were eating corn.[113]

In the Black Hills we had 10 companies, D and I Companies were at Devil's Lake.[114] We got back the last of August or the 1st of Sept.[115]

Henley says this expedition was to explore the country and verify reports of the existence of gold in the Hills and not to drive out miners.

---

[111]See the account by John E. Remsburg and George J. Remsburg, *Charlie Reynolds* (Kansas City: H. M. Lender, 1931), Chapter 5.

[112]For the story of hardships Reynolds encountered on the trip, see Custer, *Boots and Saddles*, pp. 199-201.

[113]I can find no accounts where the command had run short of rations on their way back to Ft. Lincoln. Jackson, *Custer's Gold*, pp. 98-103. Carroll and Frost, *Private Theodore Ewert's Diary*, pp. 75-77, or Frost, *With Custer in '74*, pp. 84-86. Most accounts mention, however, a shortage of water and animal feed.

[114]"On May 30 troops D and I, under command of Major Reno, again left Ft. Totten for field duty as escort to the International Northern Boundary Survey Commission. They arrived back at Ft. Totten on Sept. 14th. Lt. Col. Melbourne Chandler, *Of Garry Owen in Glory* (Annandale: Turnpike Press, 1960), pp. 41-42.

[115]The expedition arrived back at Ft. Lincoln on August 30th. Jackson, *Custer's Gold*, p. 101.

Henley Interviews: Black Hills

The expedition sent in later to drive out miners are referred to in Whittaker's book.[116]

Henley says Bailey made the boots for Reynolds' horse when Reynolds went to Laramie. (Ask Bailey about this.)[117] When we got back Charley had gone by train and was leaning against Sutler store counter.

Regarding Sitting Bull and the Battle of Little Bighorn

Henley was a 1st Sergeant in B troop from 1870 to '75 and again from '78 to '83.

He was at Standing Rock for years and was in the employ of Mrs. Galpin (she was a trader), a friend of Sitting Bull, for several years.[118] He can talk the Sioux language fluently and was intimate with Sitting Bull, Rain-In-The-Face and many other Indians who were

---

[116]See Frederick Whittaker, *A Popular Life of Gen. George A. Custer*, (N.Y: Sheldon & Co., 1876), p. 511.

[117]Saddler John E. Bailey, B Company. Born in Joe Daviess County, Illinois. Second enlistment on Dec. 10, 1875, at age 30 in Shreveport La. Discharged on Dec. 9, 1880, at Ft. Yates, Dakota. Upon expiration of service as a saddler of very good character. He had blue eyes, dark hair, dark complexion, and was 5' 11½" in height. Hammer, *Biographies*, p. 62. One account has Reynolds riding a horse with the shoes nailed on backwards. Jay Monaghan, *Custer* (Lincoln: Bison Books, 1971), p. 355. Another account, however, agrees with Henley: "... he (Reynolds) devised special leather sandals cinched with drawstrings for the horse. Pulled over the animal's iron shod hoofs, the sandals would leave tracks like those of a shoeless Indian pony." Keith Wheeler, *The Scouts* (Alexandria: Time-Life Books, 1973), p. 92

[118]Standing Rock Agency was founded in 1873 and abandoned in 1903. It was the home of Hunkpapa, Yankton, and Blackfeet Sioux. Today the present town of Ft. Yates, North Dakota, occupies its former spot. Ferris, *Soldier and Brave*, pp. 247-48. Mrs. Galpin was a Yanktonian Sioux and the wife of Major Charles Galpin, a well known Indian Trader. Mrs. Galpin was a woman of unusual character, intelligent and respected by both white and red man. Both had known Sitting Bull from the mid-1860s. Stanley Vestal, *Sitting Bull* (Norman: University of Oklahoma Press, 1965), p. 98.

Camp on Custer

present when Custer was killed and often talked with them. He thinks perhaps he had a better opportunity to talk with the Indians on this subject than any other white man and was in a good position to judge the accuracy of their stories. He was on such familiar terms with them, and then not being in military service, that they were apparently unguarded and seemingly talked to him without restraint, etc.[119]

He says Sitting Bull once told him that no one knew which Indian killed Custer. In fact, at the time of the battle the Indians did not know that Custer was present.[120]

While they supposed the soldiers to be Custer men, they thought that Custer was with the party on the bluffs (Reno). Custer had at this time his hair cut and wore the officers ordinary uniform and did not have the long hair and buckskin hunting suit as is commonly reported and hence the Indians did not recognize him from memories of his accustomed former appearance.[121]

Sitting Bull says the Indians simply knew that they had a body of soldiers cornered and that they were trying to kill them all. He says there was heavy firing and thick dust all around and much confusion of Indians,

---

[119]Henley's ability to speak the Sioux language lends a greater level of creditability to the stories he related. Too often the interviewers had to rely on interpreters and there was no way of telling how much "color" they were adding to the Indian's account.

[120]This agrees with the research done by Stanley Vestal. No one knew who killed Custer. Spotted Blackbird said "If we could have seen where each bullet landed we might have known. But hundreds of bullets were flying that day." John Stands in Timber, *Cheyenne Memories* (New Haven: Yale University Press, 1967), p. 203. It was not until some time after the battle that Sitting Bull even learned it was Custer his people fought against. Vestal, *Sitting Bull*, p. 172.

[121]For a description of Custer's dress at the Little Bighorn, see James S. Hutchins, "The Cavalry Campaign Outfit at the Little Big Horn," *Military Collector & Historian*, Winter 1956, Vol. 7, #4, pp. 91-101.

running to and fro. The excitement and confusion were so great that they wounded 40 of their own men with arrows.[122]

Henley thinks Mrs. Galpin might have been a half sister of Sitting Bull, but always thought she was a sister.[123]

Indian's supply of ammunition in 1876—Topping says they had large supplies of it when the war began in the spring of 1876, but its continual use in game hunting and a large amount of random shooting in the fight exhausted it.[124]

Henley said Sitting Bull told him that as near as he could estimate, the fighting strength of the Indians on June 25 at the Village was 5,200 guns, including warriors and armed boys and squaws who were supposed to fight if emergency required.[125] Sitting Bull says if Custer had attacked with his whole regiment, the result would have been the same—all would have been killed. He also says that after trying Reno, the Indians concluded that they would starve him out and would have done so if Terry had not come up.[126]

---

[122]"At the end it was quite a mess. They (Sioux) could not tell which was this man or that man". In fact the Sioux even scalped one of their own allies, a Cheyenne, Lame White Man. Timber, *Cheyenne Memories*, pp. 201-203. Not only were warriors wounded by arrows but several were killed by them as well. *South Dakota Historical Collections*, Vol. #6, p. 227.

[123]As stated in note #118, Mrs. Galpin was a Yanktonian. Sitting Bull was a Hunkpapa, as were his mother and father. Alexander B. Adams, *Sitting Bull* (N.Y: Putnam & Sons, 1973), p. 25. Also refer to John M. Carroll, *The Arrest and Killing of Sitting Bull* (Glendale: Arthur H. Clark Co., 1986), Appendix D, Sitting Bull Genealogy, pp. 151-56.

[124]E.S. Topping, *Chronicles of the Yellowstone* (Minneapolis: Ross & Haines, Inc., 1968). Recent archaeology research at the Custer Battlefield concluded: "When all the firearm data are taken into account, it becomes readily apparent that Custer and his men were out gunned." Scott, *Archaeological Perspectives on the Battle of the Little Big Horn*, pp.119-21.

[125]For the best discussions on the strength of the Indian village that day, see Edgar I. Stewart, *Custer's Luck* (Norman: University of Oklahoma Press, 1955), pp. 309-12.

[126]This is essentially the same story as was told to Dr. Charles Eastman, "Story of the Little Big Horn," *Chautauquan*, July 1900, Vol. 31, p. 358.

Camp on Custer

Sitting Bull said many Indians talked of the battle without knowing anything about it in particular and some had surely misstated facts.[127] No Indian knew Custer was present, but supposed that whoever the commanding officer was, he was on the hill (Reno) with the main body. He said that they understood that the men they killed were only a detachment. He said the sound of firing in the battle was as rapid as the sound of tearing a wet blanket.[128] The whole fight lasted about two hours.

Sitting Bull had utter contempt for Rain-In-The-Face and never liked him.

Regarding Sitting Bull at Standing Rock

In 1881 when Sitting Bull came down from Ft. Buford to Standing Rock, the post at Standing Rock was garrisoned by Companies H, B and K of 17th Infantry under Captains Howe, VanHorne and O'Brien and by troops B and D of 7th Cavalry[129] (B troop, Capt. McDougall, 1st Lt. John C. Gresham, and 2nd Lieut.

---

[127] About the Custer Battle the old time Sioux used to say, "There are too many tongues." Vestal, *Sitting Bull*, p. 172.

[128] Kill Eagle recounted much the same story in regard to the sound of the firing. "He described the firing...by clapping his hands together with great rapidity and regularity." Col. W. A. Graham, *The Custer Myth* (Harrisburg: Stackpole Press, 1953), p. 47.

[129] Edgar W. Howe. Born Mass. USMA, 1874. 2nd Lt., 17th Inf. 1 June 1878, 1st Lt. 30 Jan. 1885, Capt. 20 April, 1898. William McC. Van Horne. Born Ohio. 2nd Lt. and 1st Lt. 17th Inf. 23 Feb. 1866. Reg. Adj. 1 Feb. 1869 to 15 Dec. 1870. Reg. Quartermaster 15 Dec. 1870 to 24 July 1872. Capt. 31 Dec. 1872. Major 22nd Inf. 27 March 1896. Lt. Col. 18th Inf. 1 Nov. 1898. Lyster M. O'Brien. Born Mich. Capt. 27th Mich. 14 Dec. 1864. Mustered out of Vol. service 26 July, 1865. 2nd Lt. 16 Inf. 11 May 1866. Unassigned 26 April 1869. Assigned to 17th Inf. 15 Dec. 1870. Capt. 12 March 1879, Major 22 April 1898. Powell, *List of Officers*.

Henley Interviews: Sitting Bull

SITTING BULL
Taken during his confinement at Fort Randall, 1882. Photo by Bailey, Dix and Mead.
Courtesy, Paul Harbaugh Collection

Thoms. H. Barry, and D troop, Capt. Godfrey, 1st Lt. Edgerly and 2nd Lt. Brewer)[130] Col. C. C. Gilbert, 17th Infantry the commanding officer of the post.[131]

I was present when the boat carrying Sitting Bull and his band arrived.[132] Before he came off, Running

---

[130]John C. Gresham. Born Va. USMA 1873. 2nd Lt. 3rd Cav. 15 June 1876. Transferred to 7th Cav. 26 June 1876. 1st Lt. 28 June 1878. Capt. 3 April 1892. Medal of Honor for action at Wounded Knee Creek, SD, Dec. 29, 1890 while serving as 1st Lt. 7 Cav. Thomas H. Barry. Born N.Y. USMA 1873. 2nd Lt. 7th Cav. 15 June, 1877. Trans. 1st Inf. 31 Aug. 1880. 1st Lt. 1st Inf. March 1882. Capt. 25 Feb. 1891. Major A.A.G. 24 Jan. 1897. Lt. Col. A.A.G. Vol. 22 June 1898. Edwin P. Brewer. Born Ohio. USMA Cadet July 1871-Nov. 1871. 2nd Lt. 7th Cav. 31 Aug. 1876. 1st Lt. 23 Sept. 1885. Capt. 8 Dec. 1896. Powell, *List of Officers*.

[131]Charles C. Gilbert. Born Ohio. USMA 1842. 2nd Lt. 1st Inf. 27 Sept. 1846. 1st Lt. 10 June 1850. Capt. 8 Dec. 1855. Brig. Gen. U.S.V. 9 Sept. 1862 for Pittsburgh Landing, Tenn. Major 19th Inf. 2 July 1863. Transferred to 28th Inf. 21 Sept. 1866. Lt. Col. 7th Inf. 8 July 1868. Col. 17th Inf. 19 May 1881. Retired 1 March 1886. Powell, *List of Officers*.

[132]Sitting Bull arrived at Standing Rock on Aug. 1, 1881, on the steamboat *General Sherman*. Vestal, *Sitting Bull*, p. 234.

Camp on Custer

Antelope boarded the boat and went up on the hurricane deck to meet Sitting Bull who seemed to be in tears and when Antelope greeted him he said: "This is the first time I have had to surrender and give up." Running Antelope then put his arm around him and said: "Brother don't weep, everything will come out all right." [133]

Sitting Bull and his band were with us for some weeks and difficulty arose in enforcing discipline. Col. Gilbert was determined that these Indians should keep clean quarters and a police sergeant was sent around every morning with a slop cart into which the Indians were supposed to throw all of the rubbish from their teepees and the streets between them. This they finally refused to do and the sergeant complained that he could not compel the Indians to do as ordered, to which Col. Gilbert replied, "Throw the teepees and the Indians together into the slop cart and dump them into the river." The sergeant inquired: "Do you mean that I shall carry out that order?" and Col. Gilbert replied: "I say throw them and their teepees into the river. We will compel them to clean up or we will clean them up." Accordingly, the sergeant went about doing as he was ordered, tearing down a teepee and throwing it into the cart. When some of the chiefs and the interpreter came running up in protest, the sergeant said: "I have nothing to do with you, I am carrying out orders." The Indians then put up a hustle and appealed to headquarters, saying that they had not understood fully what was wanted and hereafter they would pay

---

[133]Col. William Bowen wrote "...the final surrender of his cherished independence was a hard blow to his pride, and he took it hard. He was much 'broken.'" Ibid., p. 232.

better attention to orders. Gilbert then directed the Sergeant to stop and give them a chance to obey.

The Indians were getting good rations and appeared to like their treatment well enough, but still there was discontent and it was thought best to send Sitting Bull and some of his people away, to take him from the influence of the other Indians. He was then ordered removed down the river to Ft. Randall, together with a number of his band, but this he strenuously objected to, saying that he could get along with the soldiers if they would only leave him alone.[134] He did not fear that the soldiers would lie or steal, but agents would do both and he wanted nothing to do with any of them. But his remonstrances were of no avail and the day came when he and his people had to get aboard the steamer to start for Ft. Randall. The Indians were taken to the river bank, by the steamer, with a guard of soldiers around them. Sitting Bull, who was inclined not to submit, tried to walk through the guard line. One of the sergeants pulled him back with his hand two or three times. Capt. Howe, who happened to see this, cried out: "Sergeant, are you afraid of that man? Why don't you strike him?" The Sergeant replied: "You tell me to hit him?" Howe said "Hit him" and bing went the stock of the sergeant's gun against the breast of Sitting Bull, knocking him down into a heap. Just then a soldier caught the hammer of his gun against something in some manner and his piece was discharged. The unexpected report of the gun threw everyone into a state of excitement and for the mo-

---

[134]Sitting Bull was separated from his followers and sent to Fort Randall to be held—in effect—as a prisoner of war. It wasn't until May of 1883 that he was returned to his people at the Standing Rock Agency. Adams, *Sitting Bull*, p. 350.

Camp on Custer

ment it was thought a fight had started. The officers, however, acted cooly but quickly, and the men held their fire and trouble was avoided. We did not know if some of the Indians might have arms secreted and trouble was looked for.[135]

My experience with Sitting Bull and observation of him after he returned from Ft. Randall was that he was easy to get along if treated fairly. [136]

---

[135] This is a valuable first person account of the removal of Sitting Bull from Standing Rock Agency. I am unaware of any other accounts of that episode.

[136] Buffalo Bill Cody summed it up best: "The whole secret of treating with Indians is to be honest with them and do as you agree." Vestal, *Sitting Bull*, p. 251.

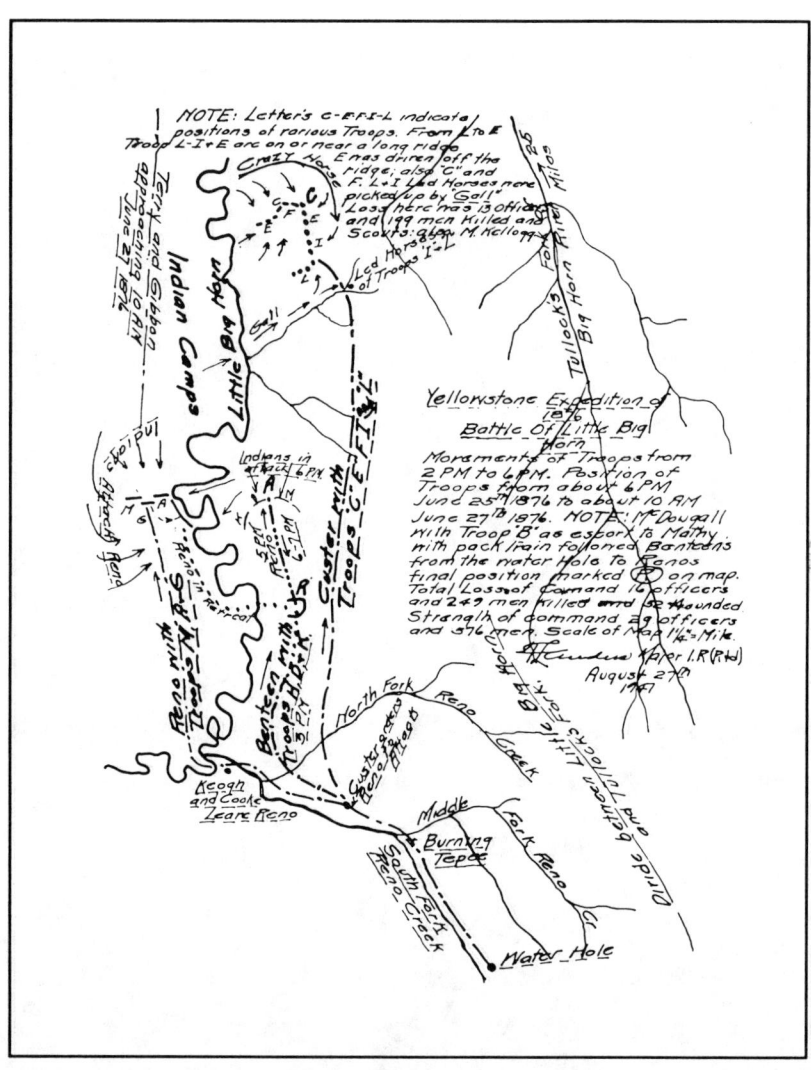

This map by Frank L. Anders shows the route of
Custer's Troops on June 25th to 27th.
Courtesy, John M. Carroll Collection

Chapter 2

7th Cavalrymen, Frontiersmen, the Battle of the Little Bighorn and other incidents

Interview with August Seifert

August Seifert, was a private in K Company. He was born in Hesse, Germany, on July 26, 1850. At the Battle of the Little Bighorn he was in his second enlistment. Lieutenant Edward Godfrey administered the oath for the second time on January 16, 1875, at Colfax, Louisiana. Seifert listed his previous occupation as baker. He was discharged on January 15, 1880, at Fort Totten, Dakota Territory, upon expiration of service as a private of excellent character. In the U.S. Army's Register of Enlistments his name is spelled "Siefort." Seifert died on February 25, 1904, in Highwood, Illinois and is buried at Fort Sheridan, Illinois.

I saw White Swan near the river and on west side, in the bottom fighting a half dozen Sioux and he was hit several times.[137] Some men ran down the bluff and fired and the Sioux withdrew. This was after Reno had retreated out of the valley, so White Swan must have retreated after Reno's men did. White Swan did not want to leave the bottom, but wanted to stay and fight.

---

[137]White Swan (Strikes Enemy) was wounded in the Valley fight. He was a Crow Indian who enlisted in the 7th Infantry on April 10, 1876, for six months. On detached service with 7th Cavalry from June 21st, accompanied Lt. Charles Varnum on the trip to the Crow's Nest, arriving there about 2:30 A.M. on June 25. He was one of ten Indian Scouts engaged in the Valley fight. He was severely wounded in the right hand after the retreat, after the ford. He died on August 12, 1904, at Crow Agency, Mont., and was interred in the Custer Battlefield National Cemetery, Grave 460a. Hammer, *Biographies*, p. 40.

Camp on Custer

He says White Swan was in the valley standing beside his horse and firing at the Sioux. He would not mount up to try to get away, but stood and fought. Half Yellow Face was across the river on the east side, afterward he helped me to get White Swan out of the bottom.[138] Half Yellow Face had not separated from White Swan on the retreat in the valley.

Sgt. Robert Hughes, who was killed with Custer, carried the Regimental flag.[139] It was yellow flag with an eagle. The colors (stars and stripes) were not carried at Little Big Horn.[140]

The flag carried by Vickory was Custer's brigade flag that he carried in the Civil War.[141]

---

[138]Half-Yellow Face was in the valley and hilltop fights. A Crow Indian scout, he enlisted in the 7th Infantry on April 10, 1876, for six months by Lt. James Bradley. He was the leader of the Crow scouts. On detached service from June 21 with the 7th Cavalry he was assigned to Major Reno's column. He accompanied Lt. Charles Varnum on the trip to the Crow's Nest, arriving there about 2:30 A.M. June 25. He was one of the ten Indian scouts who participated in the Valley fight on the skirmish line with the Reno column. Hammer, *Biographies*, p. 34. For more details on all the Crow scouts, see Graham, *The Custer Myth*, pp. 7-27.

[139]Sgt. Robert H. Hughes, K Company, was killed with the Custer Battalion on June 25. Hughes carried Custer's battle flag and was killed on Custer Hill. Born in Dublin, Ireland. Second enlistment on Oct. 1, 1873, at age 33, at Fort Rice, Dakota. He had blue eyes, brown hair, fair complexion and was 5' 9" in height. Listed as R. H. Hughes on the battle monument. Hammer, *Biographies*, p. 189. Hughes was not the regimental standard-bearer, this flag was carried rolled up and with the pack train. Col. W. A. Graham, *Westerners Brand Book, 1950,* "Custer's Battle Flags" (Los Angeles Corral of Westerners, 1950), pp. 123-36. What Hughes carried was Custer's personal flag, a red and blue swallow-tail guidon with white crossed sabers. Ibid., p. 129. Hughes was not found on Custer Hill. Capt. Thomas McDougall identified his body in a deep ravine. Hardoff, *The Custer Battle Casualties*, p. 45.

[140]The Regimental Standard from 1866 to 1887, was a blue background with a gold eagle. It was later changed to a yellow background with darker gold eagle. Chandler, *Of Garry Owen in Glory*, p. 22. This later version seems to be the one remembered by Seifert.

[141]John Vickory, Company F. Killed in battle on June 25. Born in Toronto, Canada. Second enlistment on Sept. 9, 1874, at age 27 at Ft. Lincoln. He had blue eyes, brown hair, dark complexion, and was 5' 10" in height. He was the regimental color bearer. Hammer, *Biographies*, p. 123. Private Thomas O'Neill stated Vickory lay right near Custer. Hardoff, *The Custer Battle Casualties*, p. 117. Seifert apparently confused Vickory who carried the regimental flag when it was unfurled, with Hughes who carried Custer's personal headquarters flag. Camp seemed to note some confusion here as he made the note: "Better verify this" in the interview.

Little Bighorn Interviews

Before Benteen's 3 troops got to Reno, he met 3 Crows on the bluff who were painted up.[142] Some of the men thought them hostiles, but Benteen cautioned them not to shoot, saying they were our own scouts.

Seifert says the body of Francis Hughes of L troop was found in a deep ravine with E Company men.[143] Chief Trumpeter Voss was near Custer.[144] Regarding Sergt. Robert Hughes of K Troop, his pants were found in the village.

He saw the heads of two men in village. One of them had black hair, the other red hair and was in a camp kettle.[145] Dewitt Winney and Helmer were killed in evening of 6/25.[146]

---

[142]Both Lt. Winfield S. Edgerly and Lt. Edward S. Godfrey saw these Indians on the Bluffs. James Willert, *Little Big Horn Diary* (La Mirada, CA: n.p., 1977), p. 336. For the various activities of these scouts before Capt. Frederick Benteen reached Reno Hill, see Gray, *Custer's Last Campaign*, pp. 280-84. Benteen testified before his arrival on Reno Hill "I noticed 3 or 4 Indians on my right, 400-500 yards from me, but as I approached them, I saw they were Crows..." Robert M. Utley (ed.), *The Reno Court of Inquiry* (Ft. Collins: Old Army Press, 1972), p. 321.

[143]Francis Hughes, L Company. This private was killed in battle on June 25. Born in Leavenworth, Kansas. Enlisted on May 27, 1875, at age 21 at Ft. Lincoln, Dakota. Previous occupation was laborer. He had blue eyes, brown hair, light complexion and was 5' 7¾" in height. Listed as F. F. Hughes on the battle monument. Hammer, *Biographies*, p. 212. John Foley, however, told Camp he found Hughes near Custer. Hammer, *Custer in '76*, p. 147.

[144]Henry Voss was the chief trumpeter of the regiment. He was killed in the battle June 25. Born in Hanover, Germany, third enlistment on Jan. 18, 1875, in New York City. He had blue eyes, light hair, fair complexion and was 5' 8¾" in height. Hammer, *Biographies*, p. 12. Voss's body lay across Vickory's head right near Custer, Voss's face being down. Hardoff, *The Custer Battle Casualties*, p. 117.

[145]Dr. Holmes Paulding of Terry's column recorded: "Three decapitated heads were found at the site of one of the camp fires. The hair of the skulls had been entirely burned off. Who their victims might have been would never be known." Willert, *Little Big Horn Diary*, p. 419.

[146]DeWitt Winney, K Company, First Sergeant. Killed in the hill top fight on June 25. Born Saratoga, N.Y. Enlisted on Nov. 6, 1872, at age 27 in New York City. Previous occupation was laborer. He had gray eyes, brown hair, dark complexion, and was 5' 4½" in height. Hammer, *Biographies*, p. 187. For an account of Winney's death see Edgar I. Stewart, *The Field Diary of Lt. Edward S. Godfrey* (Portland: Champoeg Press, 1957), p. 14. Julius Helmer, K. Company, killed in battle June 25. Born Hanover, Germany. Third enlistment on July 10, 1875, at age 29 in Cincinnati, Ohio. He had gray eyes, brown hair, light complexion at was 5' 9¾" in height. Hammer, *Biographies*, p. 190.

Camp on Custer

Seifert says Clear was killed on east side of river by Indians on same side.[147]

Also, Gustave Korn was with the packs when Reno started toward Custer at 5 P.M. June 25. He never heard about his going with Custer.[148]

Seifert heard about Nathan Short as soon as he got to camp, opposite the mouth of the Rosebud. He said the dead body was found by the Indian Scouts. The hat that was under body had the letter "C" on it, at the time he was thought one of Custer's men who got away badly wounded.[149]

Seifert served from 1875-1880. At Wounded Knee, Seifert said, no Indians got out of the fight alive. All were disarmed coming out of the gully. He said Big Foot was killed on a mule at Wounded Knee.

---

[147]Elihu F. Clear, K Company. Killed while climbing the bluff during the retreat from the Valley fight on June 25. He was an orderly for Dr. James DeWolf who was killed nearby. Born in Randolph County, Indiana. Second Enlistment on Jan. 4, 1871, at age 28 in Yorkville, South Carolina. He had light blue eyes, brown hair, dark complexion and was 5' 6½" in height. Hammer, *Biographies*, p. 193.

[148]Seifert was right about Korn. He was detached to Major Reno's Battalion. However, he did not rejoin Reno's command until that night (June 25). His horse bolted and was killed near the river on the retreat from the bottom, leaving Korn afoot and stranded. Gustave Korn, I Company, in the Valley and Hilltop fights. Born in Sprollow, Silesia. Enlisted on May 17, 1873, at age 21, in St. Louis. Previous occupation was a clerk. Discharged on May 17, 1878, at Ft. Lincoln, Dakota, upon expiration of service. He reenlisted and was promoted to Sergeant. Killed on Dec. 29, 1890, at Wounded Knee Creek, S.D., in an engagement with Sioux Indians of Big Foot's band. He is interred at Ft. Riley, Kansas. Hammer, *Biographies*, p. 178.

[149]This is another mention of the Nathan Short saga. An extensive review on this subject was done in Camp's interview with Frank Sniffin (10/18/1913). See pages 84-87 in this book. Seifert never saw the body, only heard about its discovery, but his recollections are almost identical to the other accounts, which claim it was indeed Nathan Short's body. Nathan Short, C Company. Killed in the battle June 25. Born in Lehigh County, Pa. Enlisted on Oct. 9, 1875, at age 21 in St. Louis. Previous occupation was a laborer. He had gray eyes, brown hair, fair complexion and was 5' 7" in height. Hammer, *Biographies*, p. 84.

Little Bighorn Interviews

Interview with John Lattman

John Lattman was a private in G Company,. He was born in Zurich, Switzerland, in 1848. He enlisted on Oct. 14, 1873, at age 25, in Philadelphia. His previous occupation was laborer. He was discharged at Ft. Abraham Lincoln, Dakota Territory, upon expiration of service as a private of excellent character. He had gray eyes, auburn hair, ruddy complexion and was 5' 6¾" in height. Listed in records both as Lattman and Lattmann. Following his discharge he homesteaded on 160 acres of land 12 miles northeast of Rapid City, South Dakota. He remained a bachelor and died in Rapid City on October 7, 1913.

The carbine on Custer battlefield was found by George White Bear in 1890.

Is he sure Alex Brown was acting first Sgt. instead of Botzer?[150] Yes.

Did he know Thos. W. Goldin and was he one of those left in the timber? He did not see Goldin there.

Was there a bugler in timber? Don't know.

In timber were there any men of Company G whom he did not know? No.

---

[150] Alexander Brown, G Company, born in Aberdeen, Scotland, on Feb. 19, 1844. Second enlistment on Dec. 13, 1871, at age 26 in Spartanburg, S.C. Discharged on Dec. 13, 1876, at Ft. Lincoln, upon expiration of service, as a private of very good character. Reenlisted as a sergeant of troop H 7th Cavalry and died April 7th, 1884, and is interred in Ft. Meade Post Cemetery, Grave 1-44. Hammer, *Biographies*, p. 139. Edward Botzer, G Company. Killed at the ford in the retreat from the Valley fight on June 25. Born in Bremerhaven, Germany. Second enlistment on Nov. 26, 1871, at age 26 in Spartanburg, S.C. In his previous enlistment he had been a corporal in Company G. He had blue eyes, brown hair, fair complexion and was 5' 6½" in height. Hammer, *Biographies*, p. 139. Botzer is the likely candidate for "Custer's Last Trooper," a documentary which was presented on television in 1990. Dr. Monte Kloberdanz found his skull on the banks of the Little Big Horn in June 1989.

Camp on Custer

Were Benj. Johnson and Walter O. Taylor left in timber? Yes.[151]

Left in the timber were:

Lattman, John	W. O. Taylor
Petring, Henry	Weiss, Markus
McCormick, Samuel	Johnson, Benj.
McGonigle, Hugh	White, Chas, M Company
And. J. Moore	Sivertsen, John, M Company

Carey N. Weaver, M Company

Two men of A Company who did not go out

(Lattman verifies that this list as far as G Company men are concerned.)[152]

Botzer was Company quartermaster at Little Big Horn. Lattman is sure Alex Brown was acting First Sergeant. He died in Ft. Meade about 1907. I [W.M.C.] am convinced Lattman is right.

John Rapp was holding Lattman's and McIntosh's

---

[151] Benjamin Johnson, G Company. Born in Lancaster, Pa. Enlisted on June 22, 1875, at age 29 in Pittsburgh, Pa. Previous occupation was carpenter. Discharged on June 22, 1880 at Box Elder Creek, Montana, upon expiration of service as a sergeant of excellent character. He had hazel eyes, dark brown hair, dark complexion and was 5' 5½" in height. Hammer, *Biographies*, p. 144. Walter O. Taylor, G. Company. He was the company blacksmith. Born in Scituate, R.I. Enlisted in Nov. 22, 1875 at age 21 in Boston. Previous occupation was horse shoer. Discharged on Nov. 21 1880 at Newport, Ky., upon expiration of service as a blacksmith of good character. In 1927 he resided in Whitman, Mass. He had gray eyes, light hair, fair complexion and was 5' 6¾" in height. Hammer, *Biographies*, p. 142

[152] Camp was trying to establish how many men had been abandoned in the timber after Reno's order to "charge for the bluffs." No one yet has been able to tell for certain how many of his battalion remained in the timber. Willert states at least 17 men were left behind, the vast majority were G company. Willert, *Little Big Horn Dairy*, p. 322. John Gray put together the available evidence and concluded thirteen men were left in the timber for one hour, four were left in the timber until June 27th and twenty were missing—period. John S. Gray, *Centennial Campaign* (Ft. Collins: Old Army Press, 1976), p. 296. Steward wrote: "Behind him Reno left his dead and wounded, no effort being made to take them out, and he also deserted Lt. McIntosh, several scouts and from twelve to fifteen troops." Stewart, *Custer's Luck*, p. 364. With Camp's attention to every detail, he was not only trying to determine how many remained, but their names as well.

horses besides his own.[153] Dose was orderly for Custer and killed with him.[154]

Robb's horse was hit while they were in the bottom before he dismounted. During the fight on the skirmish line, it was shot in the left hind leg and made lame.[155]

Lattman says that on the skirmish line the Indians were shooting too high and they got around to our rear and we had orders to mount up. I could not find my horse. Everybody took the first horse he could get, and got out in a hurry.[156]

After all had gone, except the dismounted men, we got together and I thought someone ought to look to see if any Indians were coming in after us. There was an A Company man, brown hair, 22 or 23 years old, medium size man.[157] I said to him, "What's the use of

---

[153] John Rapp, G Company. Killed in the Valley fight on June 25. He was the orderly for Lt. Donald McIntosh and was killed while holding the horses. Born in Wurtemberg, Germany. Enlisted on Sept. 29, 1873, at age 25 in Philadelphia. Previous occupation was tanner. He had blue eyes, dark hair, fair complexion and was 5' 5¼" in height. Hammer, *Biographies*, p. 148.

[154] Henry C. Dose, G Company. Killed in battle on June 25. Born in Holstein, Germany. Second enlistment on Feb. 1, 1875, at age 25 in Shreveport, La. Previous occupation was artificer. Dose was previously enlisted in the 3rd Infantry. He had gray eyes, brown hair, fair complexion and was 5' 6" in height. His widow married First Sergeant Edward Garlick. Hammer, *Biographies*, p. 141. Henry Dose was Custer's orderly on June 25. Hammer, *Custer in '76*, p. 99. His body was found just south of Deep Ravine, a short distance from the Little Bighorn River. Hardoff, *The Custer Battle Casualties*, p. 112.

[155] Eldorado S. Robb, G company. Born in Warren County, Ky. Enlisted on Jan. 8, 1872, at age 21 in Louisville, Ky. Previous occupation was laborer. Discharged on Jan. 8, 1877, at Ft. Lincoln upon expiration of service as a private of good character. He had hazel eyes, brown hair, ruddy complexion and was 5' 9¾" in height. Hammer, *Biographies*, p. 148.

[156] For an authoritative account of the troopers scrambling to find their horses and the resultant panic see Willert, *Little Big Horn Diary*, pp. 300-303.

[157] There are three possible candidates for the A Company trooper who joined up with Lattman. They are James Drinan, James McDonald and Thomas Sweetser. Their ages and heights were 23, 5' 7"; 23, 5' 6"; 26, 5' 7" respectively. Unless more information is uncovered, it is impossible to learn which one of the three it was. Hammer, *Biographies*, pp. 44-56. In Camp's interview with Hugh McGonigle, he stated, he (McGonigle) along with Lattman and Andrew Moore and 3 others McGonigle couldn't remember, were in the timber after the retreat. Hammer, *Custer in '76*, p. 152.

Camp on Custer

sitting here waiting for Indians to rout us out. I will go to the edge of the timber and if the other men start to move, you let me know." I went and peeped out and saw half dozen Indians going over east, in the direction Reno had retreated. I went back and everybody but him was gone, and I asked where they had gone and he said they had gone looking for the command. I was angry and scolded him. We sat there quite a long while and about 6 loose horses came around and we caught them and tied them up. They all belonged to my company and had come back to timber after their riders had been killed in the retreat to the river. We identified them as such. All at once the horses began to pick up their ears and look, but we could see nothing and I said we will have to look out and the Indians must be coming.

I held my carbine in readiness to shoot, when an Indian rode into the timber, but the Indian could not see me. I decided not to shoot unless he tried to shoot me. All at once he saw me and was so frightened he nearly fell off his pony and quickly turned and rode away.

I then said to the A Company man, "I guess we will have to move now, as the Indian will tell the others about us." I took Lt. McIntosh's horse and the other man took a horse, and I got on and could not use the stirrups as McIntosh had longer legs than I. We had been hearing firing down where Custer was and when we were mounted we started to go down that way and we crossed the Little Big Horn, the A Company man following me.[158] When we got out in the open on the

---

[158]Frederick Gerard, also in the timber heard firing from Custer's battalion about 15 minutes after Reno retreated. Ron Nichols, *Reno Court of Inquiry* Vol. II (Costa Mesa, CA: n.p., 1983), pp. 108-109. The two men must have crossed the Little Bighorn somewhere across from the Weir Point area.

Little Bighorn Interviews

east side, we thought we saw soldiers on the bluffs (They were on the same flat as Thompson and Watson).[159] We were on the flat across from the timber on open prairie. When we got half way to bluffs, we could see a red blanket on a horse and knew it was an Indian and turned to go back to the river. The Indians fired at me and my horse jumped. Having no stirrups, I nearly fell off and we put back for the timber on the west side. When we got on other side, I ran against a bank so steep I could not get the horse out. I tried to get him out for some time and expected the Indians should be right after us. I left the horse in the river and went up into the thick bush. The A Company man went 20 rods further up the river where the bank was not so steep and got his horse up and mounted when an Indian in the brush on same side of river shot him off his horse and I saw him fall, but no more. He was shot about halfway between the timber and where Reno forded (Must be the man with clothes on him).

I then hid in lowly sage brush and got my carbine and pistol ready for defense. All at once I heard Indians trying to get my horse where I had left him. I laid there until dark and then started toward Custer. Again when half way up the bluff, all of a sudden, I heard Indian bells and looked and saw two Indians riding along and began to wonder where they came from and lay down to think it over and made up my mind they

---

[159]From the appearance of Camp's written notes on this interview, Lattman did not speak these words. Camp wrote this as a memo to himself to understand the part of the battlefield where the two troopers were now located. Camp had consistently over the years, through his interviews, inquired about three people who greatly perplexed him—Goldin, Thompson and Watson, especially the latter two. See map on the frontispiece of Daniel O. Magnussen, *Peter Thompson's Narrative of the Little Big Horn Campaign 1876* (Glendale: Arthur H. Clark Co., 1974).

Camp on Custer

had been watching the command and I started and walked that way. I walked along quite a distance and got into a ravine and looked up and saw a pony. Soon I saw a man whom I took for a soldier and as I walked up he challenged me and told me where camp was. I had been out nearly all night and it was nearly daylight when I joined the command on the hill.[160]

In burying the dead the smell was so bad we had to be relieved every 5 minutes.[161] McIntosh and McCormick's horses lay together. He had only a calico shirt on when his body was found.[162] I was one of those who pushed for water on June 26.[163]

---

[160] In the many accounts of the battle, there is no mention of Lattman arriving at Reno Hill before daylight on the 26th. In particular see Willert, *Little Big Horn Diary*, p. 368 and 390-94.

[161] For a graphic description of the battlefield stench and conditions refer to Francis B. Taunton, *Custer's Field* (London, England: Johnson-Taunton Military Press, 1984), p. 22.

[162] Lattman is most accurate here. Thomas O'Neill explained further to Camp that he "...passed McIntosh going out on McCormick's horse. McIntosh asked me where Reno's command was. I next passed Rapp who was leading McIntosh's horse. Rapp inquired for *Tosh*. The Indians soon came up and killed Rapp." Hammer, *Custer in '76*, p. 107. Col. John Gibbon recorded that McIntosh was identified by one of the officers who recognized an article of clothing on the partially clad body. Col. John Gibbon "Last Summer's Expedition Against The Sioux," *American Catholic Quarterly Review*, Oct. 1977, vol. II, p. 300. Through Lattmann we now know it was a calico shirt which aided in identifying the remains. The officer who recognized the shirt was McIntosh's brother-in-law, Lt. Francis Gibson of H Company.

[163] Lattman claims he rushed for water on June 26. However, he was not remembered as one who did, see Camp's extensive notes on the water parties. Refer to pages 110-13 in this book. But this would not preclude Lattman from going to the river by himself to obtain water and no one recognizing him for the act.

Interview with John A. Bailey

John E. Bailey was a saddler in B Company. He was born in 1845 in Joe Daviess County, Illinois. He reenlisted on December 10, 1875, in Shreveport, Louisiana. John was discharged on December 9, 1890, at Fort Yates, Dakota Territory, upon expiration of service as a saddler of very good character. He is listed as John A. Bailey in the Register of Enlistments, U.S. Army.

Bailey says that on June 25, McDougall was to have the advance, but he was asleep when Custer had officers call and Custer, hearing of this, told him he would have to take the rear guard that day.[164] Bailey says some of the Company wept when they learned this. Bailey states that Boss Custer did not get back to the pack train. He said if he exchanged horses, he must have done it in advance of the pack train.[165]

(Query: How does Bailey know this, he being with the rear guard?)

Hodgson's body was found on the bank at the edge of the river. He had been stripped by the Indians before being found on the night of June 26. His body was buried about 40 or 50 feet up the hill from Mc-

---

[164] This is a different account of how B Company was assigned to guard the pack train. According to the majority of participants, after Custer had returned from the Crow's Nest, he informed the company commanders what he wanted and the first to report "ready" would have the advance. Benteen's H Company reported "ready" ahead of the others and was given the honor. Willert, *Little Big Horn Diary*, p. 262.

[165] This does not agree with what Captain Thomas McDougall told Walter Camp. The Captain stated he "saw and talked with Boston Custer when he came back to the pack train." Perhaps Bailey missed seeing the youngest Custer before he left to join his brothers in battle and death. Hammer, *Custer in '76*, p. 69.

Camp on Custer

Dougall's entrenchment under a little bush-like tree, which is no longer there, on the night of June 26.[166]

Bailey says Coleman and Spinner were the first to go for water.[167]

Trumble was the orderly for Hodgson and was the second man to get to the top of the bluffs on the retreat, Reno having been first.[168]

None of the bodies around Custer's had been scalped, but one.

Hodgson lay with his feet in the river, says Bailey.

He heard of a man found near the Rosebud and thinks it was one of Crook's men.[169]

Callan and a man from Second Company left Major Brisbin to carry a message to Miles at Fort Keogh.[170] After eight or ten miles, Callan's horse gave out and Callan took it (the horse) afoot down the Tongue and

---

[166]It would appear just as many people remember burying Lt. Hodgson as remember helping him after he was wounded. Captain McDougall told Camp: "The men who recovered Hodgson's body on the night of June 26 were Criswell, Private Ryan and Saddler Bailey, all of B Troop." Hammer, *Custer in '76*, p. 72. Also see Jud Tuttle, "Who Buried Lieutenant Hodgson?," *4th Annual Symposium*, June 22, 1990, pp. 9-17 and Bruce R. Liddic, *I Buried Custer* (College Station: Young West, 1979), p. 20.

[167]For a full length biography of Thomas W. Coleman, see Liddic, Ibid. Private Philipp Spinner, B Company. Born in Baden, Germany. Enlisted on December 12, 1870, at age 24 at Fort Leavenworth. Second enlistment December 12, 1875, at Shreveport, Louisiana. After his fourth enlistment in 1886, he was transferred to the 3rd Cavalry. His fifth enlistment was on January 25, 1891. He had gray eyes, light brown hair, ruddy complexion and was 5' 6½" in height. He committed suicide in Wisconsin in 1894. Hammer, *Biographies*, p. 71.

[168]Private William Trumble, B Company. Born in Iowa, enlisted September 9, 1873, at age 21 in Cincinnati. Previous occupation was laborer. Fourth enlistment was on January 26, 1889, at Fort Sill where he was assigned to Troop C, 8th Cavalry. He had gray eyes, brown hair, florid complexion and was 5' 8" in height. He was illiterate. Ibid., p. 72

[169]For a different viewpoint of the body found on the Rosebud, see Camp's interview with Frank Sniffin, herein.

[170]Private Thomas J. Callan, B Company. Born in Louth, Ireland. Enlisted on March 10, 1876, at age 22 in Boston. Discharged March 9, 1881, at Fort Yates, Dakota, upon expiration of service as a private of good character. He had blue eyes, dark hair, fair complexion and was 5' 9½" in height. Awarded the Medal of Honor October 24, 1896, for gallantry as a member of the water party. He died March 6, 1906, in Yonkers, NY. Hammer, *Biographies*, p. 64.

Little Bighorn Interviews

the other man went on and carried the dispatch to Miles and said nothing about Callan. This dispatch was from Major Brisbin who had four troops of the Second Cavalry and B Company of the Seventh Cavalry up the Tongue. Bailey says the dispatch was not from_____ [Illegible] as commonly reported.

Inquire Bailey:
What Companies on Reno Scout?
    B and H, B and I[171]
Just where did Hodgson fall?
    Edge of water.
Was H. Chapman transferred from B to E in June?[172]
Was he at Little Big Horn?
    Don't know.
Gustov Korn story?
    Never heard of it.
Don't remember what company was rear guard June 24.

He says B Company was on Reno scout and also I Company. Mitch Bouyer was the only scout with Reno that he could remember.[173]

He says that the night Reno turned back, Mitch told Reno he could take him to the Sioux village in two hours' time. Reno said he did not wish to see it.[174]

---

[171]The companies on the Reno scout were B, C, E, F, I and L.

[172]This was William E. Chapman. He was transferred from B to E Company on June 1, 1876, per Special Order #49. He deserted on October 15, 1876. He had gray eyes, dark hair, ruddy complexion and was 5' 9¼" in height. Hammer, *Biographies*, p. 113.

[173]In addition to Mitch Bouyer, Reno was furnished with eight Arikara scouts. Edgar I. Stewart and Major E.S. Luce, "The Reno Scout," *Montana*, Summer 1960, vol. 10, #3, p. 23.

[174]Willert suggests that Reno might have gone further, but his rations were running out. Willert, *Little Big Horn Diary*, p. 173.

Reno's scouts had reached a point about 35 miles from the Indian village. Thus it would have taken considerably more than two hours for the command to reach the hostiles. Gray, *Custer's Last Campaign*, pp. 191-192.

Camp on Custer

Bailey says Mitch had been out ahead and seen the village, but this I [Camp] doubt.

Bailey says Richard A. Wallace was drowned on picket July 25, 1876.[175] Sergeant Wilson said he (Wallace) tried to cross a coulee filled with a rushing torrent which had followed a hard rain. His (Wallace's) horse got across, but he was drowned. He was on his way to his picket post.

Wallace had been on picket across a dry coulee the night before. During the night, rain filled the coulee and when Wallace returned in the morning the water was up to his saddle girth. Wallace said, "I guess I will get drowned going back to the post" and he was. The horse got to the other bank and was not drowned. Wallace's body was never found.

Interview with Frank Sniffin
October 16, 1913,[176] Chattanooga, Tennessee
Regarding James Watson and Nathan Short

Private Sniffin, Company M, carried the company colors in the Valley fight. He was born in New York City in 1853 and was enlisted Sept. 1, 1875, at age 22 in St. Louis by Capt. Owen Hale.

---

[175] Private Richard A. Wallace, B. Company. Born in Boston. Enlisted on December 7, 1874, at age 22 in Boston. Previous occupation was teamster. Drowned on July 25, 1876, near the mouth of the Big Horn river while crossing a stream to go picket guard. He had gray eyes, dark hair, sallow complexion and was 5' 7½" in height. Hammer, *Biographies*, p. 72.

[176] Camp conducted a number of interviews in the year 1913. He started out on Jan. 16 with Lt. Burkhardt; Jan. 18, J. J. Peate; Jan. 20, Lt. Baldwin; Jan. 20, O. A. P. Wiggins; Jan. 25, Lt. Varnum, Ed LeBain and Eli Ziegler; Jan. 26, George Young and Ed Picard; Jan. 29, Starr Maxwell and Sam Morris; Feb. 5, Walter Sterland; Feb. 6, Running Wolf; Feb. 12, Margaret Bowman; June 15, Mary Collins; Sept. 18, Finn Burnett; Sept. 28, Bernard Prevo; Sept. 30, Curly; and Oct. 13, Frank Sniffin. Hammer, *Custer in '76*, pp. 6-9.

Little Bighorn Interviews

Sergeant Miles F. O'Hara,
Company M
Courtesy, Little Bighorn Battlefield National Monument

Previous occupation was laborer. He was discharged on Aug. 31, 1880, at Fort Meade, Dakota Territory, upon expiration of service as a private of good character.

James Watson

Geo. W. Weaver of my Company (M) was called "Cully" for a nickname.[177]

Sgt. O'Hara[178] was killed on our line in the bottom

---

[177]George Weaver was born in Lancaster, Pa. Second enlistment on March 15, 1876, at age 35 at Fort Rice, Dakota Territory, by Capt. Thomas French. Discharged on March 14, 1881, at Fort Meade, Dakota Territory, upon expiration of service as a farrier of excellent character. He died Oct. 14, 1886, and was interred in the Post Cemetery at Fort Meade. Grave 1-65. He had blue eyes, brown hair, florid complexion and was 5' 7" in height. Hammer, *Biographies*, p. 237. The nickname of "Cully" was again verified by Ferdinand Widmayer in Camp's interview of Oct. 7, 1910. Widmayer went on to say he was called "Cully" Weaver—to distinguish him from Trumpeter Henry C. Weaver of the same company. Hammer, *Custer in '76*, p. 145.

[178]Miles F. O'Hara was born in Alton, Ohio, enlisted on Oct. 30, 1872, at 21½ years of age in New York City, by Capt. Charles Wikoff. Previous occupation was laborer. Promoted to Sergeant in June 1876. He had gray eyes, light hair, ruddy complexion and was 5' 8¾" in height. He was reported to have been killed by a shot through the breast on the skirmish line in the Valley Fight. William Slaper told E. A. Brininstool "It was on this line that I saw the first one of my own company comrades fall. This was Sgt. O'Hara." Hammer, *Biographies*, p. 223.

Camp on Custer

and was dead or supposed to be when we left the firing line.[179]

I knew James Watson of C Company and he once told me that he went with Custer and the five companies very near to the place there, where these companies were wiped out.[180] He told me the whole story of how he came back and joined Reno. I do not recall that he ever told me about Pete Thompson being with him and I never heard Thompson tell it.[181] (Sniffin told me [W.M.C] the above before I had mentioned to him the name of either Thompson or Watson).

Nathan Short

Before I [W.M.C.] had a chance to bring up the subject of Nathan Short, Sniffin told me that in August, while Terry was marching up the Rosebud, a dead soldier and a dead horse were found near the Rosebud. He says that the body was identified as that

---

[179] It is interesting to note the comment "was dead or supposed to be." While Slaper, Rutten and Wilber, among others, claim O'Hara was killed, Edward Pigford stated that when he left the skirmish line, O'Hara called to him, "For God's sake don't leave me." But the skirmish line was no sooner formed than it broke up. Ibid., p. 143. 1st Sgt. Ryan claimed afterwards that the body was never found. Thus, O'Hara was not brought off from the place where he fell whether alive or dead. Richard G. Hardoff, *Custer Battle Casualties*, p. 142. Perhaps Sniffin has touched on another sore point, not only were men abandoned in the timber, but on the skirmish line as well.

[180] James Watson, born in Hudson, N.Y., enlisted on Sept. 10, 1875, at age 25 by Lt. Patrick Cusack. Previous occupation was laborer. In the march to the Little Bighorn River, Watson's horse became exhausted at about the time Peter Thompson's horse gave out. Watson joined Reno's command on the hill. Discharged Sept. 9, 1880, at Fort Meade, Dakota Territory, upon expiration of service as a private of very good character. He had blue eyes, brown hair, fair complexion and was 5' 6" in height. Hammer, *Biographies*, p. 86. For the stories of both Watson and Thompson, see Magnussen, *Peter Thompson's Narrative*. For an interesting story on Watson—but historically worthless—see John W. Ely, Jr. "There Was Not A Finer Lad in the Regiment," *The Baker Street Journal*, June 1982, Vol. 32, #2, pp. 82-88.

[181] For one possible reason why both Watson and Thompson kept quiet on their adventure, see Hammer, *Custer in '76*, pp. 125-126.

of Oscar T. Warner of Tom Custer's company.[182] He says his name was in his hat.

He says the matter was well discussed among the enlisted men that night. Sniffin did not see the remains. He does not recall all the details, but recalls that the man had a dead horse and that the man had been wounded.[183]

John Bruguier

John Bruguier was a half-breed, Santee Sioux, known among the Indians as "Big Leggins." He was one of thirteen children born to Theophile Bruguier and his Santee Sioux wives. He was born in

---

[182] Oscar T. Warner was born in Berne, N.Y. Enlisted on Oct. 8, 1875, at age 35 in St. Louis by Lt. John Thompson. Previous occupation was carpenter. He had blue eyes, brown hair, fair complexion and was 5' 5¾" in height. Ibid., p. 86.

[183] This is the most interesting piece of information contained in the interview. Ever since the discovery of a soldier on the Rosebud the name of Nathan Short has been associated exclusively with the remains. Now a new identity is put forth—Oscar Warner. The reason why Short's name has been linked to the remains since this discovery, was due in the large part to Daniel Kanipe's interviews and letters to Camp.

Kanipe claimed he knew it was Short and said so, even though he personally never saw the body or the horse. This was because the equipment was marked with the number 50. This was Short's unofficial service number in C Company and he had marked his gear with it. The same number 50 was found on the equipment as well as on a "white wool hat with brass crossed saber and a brass letter C," which was brought into camp and displayed. Hammer, *Custer in '76*, p. 137. Among the others agreeing with Kanipe were Richard Thompson, Ibid., p. 248, E. S. Godfrey see Graham, *The Custer Myth*, p. 146. Jacob Adams, Hammer, *Custer in '76*, p.126, Roman Rutten, Ibid., p. 120. However, Ferdinand Widmayer stated the body he and others saw at the Rosebud, was supposed to be Short's, but had been dead a long time. Thus, it could not have been he. Widmayer doesn't offer an opinion of whose body it was. Ibid., p. 146. Robert C. Doran concludes the body was Short's and he had been the messenger Curley said that Custer dispatched from Medicine Tail Coulee on a sorrel-roan horse (Company C's colors) heading north. "The Man Who Got to the Rosebud," *First Annual Symposium*, June 26, 1987, pp. 19-23.

We know a white wool hat was passed around to see if anyone could identify the owner, most witnesses claim it was Short's. Sniffin claims it was Warner's because his name was in it. Who's right? One thing for certain it belonged to a man from C Company. But Short's or Warner's?

Camp on Custer

1849 and had a long and distinguished career as a scout, guide and interpreter. Today he is largely unknown except to western history enthusiasts. With the frontier settled, John engaged in ranching and was murdered near Poplar, Montana, on June 25, 1898, while driving his wagon home along a lonely road.

Miles first met John Bruguier on Cedar Creek as a messenger from Sitting Bull and as Sitting Bull's interpreter at the meeting between the lines. Miles said to Bruguier "You are an intelligent man, what are you doing here among these hostiles?" Bruguier then told him that he had gotten into trouble and had gone among the Indians as a fugitive to escape punishment.[184] Miles wanted Bruguier to stay with him, and as Sitting Bull had already asked Bruguier to do the same for the purpose of leading Miles' command into a trap he could remain without creating Sitting Bull's suspicion and he did remain. Miles assured Bruguier that he would protect him all he could and would see that he was not arrested by the officers of the law while with him on the campaign.[185]

(Bruguier about killing of the Sioux by Crows at Ft. Keogh)

John Bruguier and Billy Cross had been sent out to

---

[184] Bruguier was charged with manslaughter along with his brother Billy in the killing of William McGee, an employee of Standing Rock Agency on Dec. 14, 1875. *Bismarck Tribune*, Dec. 22, 1875. Brother Billy served seven years of a ten year sentence, receiving a pardon from the Governor of Dakota in 1887. *Dakota Journal*, Jan. 7, 1882. With an outstanding warrant for his arrest, John fled to Sitting Bull's camp for protection in August 1876. He remained with them until he met Miles between the lines as stated in this interview. This was on October 20, 1876. John S. Gray, "What Made Johnnie Bruguier Run," *Montana Magazine of Western History*, April 1964, vol. 14, #2, pp. 34-49.

[185] General Nelson Miles needed Bruguier, as he thought Bruguier to be the best guide he could find. Thus when Miles heard his side of what happened to McGee, Miles vowed he would do all he could to help John, if he would join his campaign against Sitting Bull. Wheeler, *The Scouts*, p. 107.

talk with the camp. John Bruguier had told them that if they surrendered they would not be punished. After this, Billy Cross had told them that if they surrendered they would be punished. To ascertain the truth they decided to send a delegation of 7 men into the post to talk over the matter and told Cross to tell their commander to see that the Crow scouts made no trouble. Cross went in and did not do this but said the Sioux would be there at a certain date (which was later than the Sioux had appointed). Thus the Sioux came in unexpectedly and the Crows killed them. Bruguier says Miles was wrathy and compelled the Crows to swim the Yellowstone when anchor ice was running, and strike out for home on the Stillwater.

[Camp asked Bruguier about a number of different points and received these answers (ed.)]

Bruguier says Hump had his thigh broken in Custer fight and was shot through the shoulder at Bears Paw.[186]

On the Yellowstone Expedition 1873 Bruguier gave me the above (following list of scouts):[187]

Louis Azard	Frank Gates
Mitch Bouyer	Geor. Flenery
John Bruguier	Antoine Claymore
Nick Cadatte	Charles Reynolds

Mrs. Nunan: She had been known around the post

---

[186] Hump was a Minneconjou Dakota Chief who was 34 years old at the time of the Little Big Horn. He fought both Reno and Custer. James McLaughlin, *My Friend the Indian* (Seattle: Superior Publishing Co., 1970), p. 40. Other accounts have Hump shot in the leg. P. J. Powell, *People of the Sacred Mountain* (N.Y: Harper & Row, 1980), p. 78.

[187] Although his name, John Bruguier, appears on the list Sam Bruguier gave Camp, it does not appear in the army records of the 1873 expedition. John Gray noted, however, "There is evidence that John, having resigned his agency job on May 31, 1873, accompanied the expedition." Gray, "What Made Johnnie Bruguier Run?" p. 39.

as Widow Nash and had acted as midwife to some of the officers families says Bruguier.[188]

Billy Cross was a half breed Minneconjou. In his talks with Bruguier about the Little Big Horn he always told of being in the fight with Reno in the bottom.[189]

I asked Bruguier: Does "Palami" mean Rees or Crees?

It means "Ree."

How many in Sioux is "Tona?" One of the head chiefs of Minneconjou at the Little Big Horn was Black Moon.[190] John Grass is a Sihaspa (Blackfoot Sioux). Kill Eagle (Wambli Kte) was a Blackfoot Sioux.[191] The Ghost Dance Hump was a warrior of the Minneconjou of Little Big Horn notoriety. He was from Cherry Creek on the Cheyenne River Reservation.

Bruguier says the Sioux name for Cree is "Hcahcatway." Sioux name for "Big Horn" is "Big Horn." Sioux name for Yellowstone is "Elk River."

---

[188] There are more than a few stories about the famous Mrs. Noonan, a man who assumed the role of a woman at Ft. Lincoln. One of the better accounts of this man/woman and her husband is James Schneider, *An Enigma Named Noonan* (n.p.: n.p., 1988). Also refer to *Army-Navy Journal*, Nov. 9, 1878, article entitled "Married to a Man."

[189] William Cross—Half-blood Dakota Sioux Indian Scout. Third enlistment at age 22 on April 17, 1876, in the 7th Cavalry for six months. He may have participated in herding the captured Sioux ponies on June 25th. He told his story to a news correspondent on July 4, 1876, and is in the Chicago *Tribune*, July 15, 1876. Hammer, *Biographies*, p. 32. Cross died in 1894 on the Fort Peck Reservation near Culbertson, Montana. Stanislaus Roy told Camp, however, "...that Bob Jackson and Billy Cross never forded at Ford A. No one remembers seeing them in the valley fight or on west side of the river at all." Hammer, *Custer in '76*, p. 111.

[190] Black Moon - Hunkpapa Teton Dakota. War leader of the Fox Warrior Society, fought Reno in the valley then joined in the fight with Custer. He was killed shortly after crossing the Middle Ford. George Hyde, *Red Cloud Folk* (Norman: University of Oklahoma Press, 1967), pp. 268-70.

[191] Kill Eagle—David Miller claims he was an Ogallala Sioux and fought both Reno and Custer. Miller relates a rather lengthy account of this warrior and his actions that day. David H. Miller, *Custer's Fall* (N.Y: Duell, Sloan and Pearce, 1957), pp. 102-110.

Running Antelope was a Hunkpapa (Tatoka Inyanka). He lived at the Grand River Agency and was so peaceably inclined toward the whites that some of the Indians sought to kill him.

Bruguier says the Indians made saddles by using shoulder blades or other bones or elk horns for trees and covering them with rawhide and badger or other skins. Mont Bray first told me about this method of making saddles.

Inquire—Sam Bruguier name of brother of John Bruguier who had a part in the killing of McGee?[192] Billy.

Interview with David McVeigh
June 11, 1911

David McVeigh was a trumpeter in A Company. He was born in Philadelphia, Pennsylvania, in 1851, which was also the city from which he enlisted on October 29, 1872. His previous occupation was musician. He was discharged on June 24, 1877, at camp on Tongue River, Montana Territory, as a trumpeter of excellent character.

Says that in the bottom he held DeRudio's horse and "Hardy," Moylan's horse. I gave DeRudio his horse but don't know how it got away from him.[193]

While they were holding the horses in the timber,

---

[192]Billy Bruguier was one of John's six brothers. We have already mentioned his conviction and sentence in a previous footnote. For a full account of this affair see Gray, "What Made Johnnie Bruguier Run?" pp. 46-50.

[193]The horses held by McVeigh were those of Lt. Charles DeRudio and Capt. Myles Moylan, whose nickname among the enlisted men of A Company was "Hardy."

McVeigh could not understand how DeRudio's horse got away. DeRudio explained to Camp that "...he led his horse to the edge of the timber and decided to ride through the Indians and overtake command... He was just trying to mount his frightened and trembling horse and had his foot in stirrup when a buck jumped out of the bush and fired... frightening both DeRudio and the horse, and the horse broke away." Hammer, *Custer in '76*, p. 85.

Camp on Custer

the Indians had gotten around part of them and were setting fire to the brush. Says Sgt. Fehler had charge of A Company's hocks.[194]

On night of June 25, the Indians were blowing bugles (taken from Custer's dead soldiers) all night long, perhaps trying to deceive the soldiers on the hill. The trumpeters would sound calls, knowing that if the bugles were being blown by Custer's men they would answer, but no answers came and we knew the bugles were being blown by the Indians by the sounds they made.[195]

On way over to bury the dead on 6/28 we found two dead soldiers down in the hollow near river, about a mile from the dead on Custer Ridge. Voss lay between Lt. Cooke and McCarthy of L Co. He was not farther from Cooke than 12 feet.[196] Hughes of L Co. lay right near E Co. men, down at the gully.[197]

He says "Vic" was a sorrel horse with white feet and blaze face. Dandy was a bay horse.

---

[194]Sergeant Henry Fehler of A Company. Born in Hanover, Germany. Enlisted on Aug. 14, 1872, at age 35 in St. Louis. Previous occupation was laborer. Discharged on June 24, 1877, at camp on the Tongue River, Montana, as a private of fair character. He had blue eyes, light hair, fair complexion and was 5' 8½" in height. Hammer, *Biographies*, p. 47. "Hocks" was a slang expression, at the time, for horses.

[195]Not only did the troopers hear trumpet calls that night, but "...the wildest confusion prevailed. Men imagined they could see a column of troops over the hills, that they could hear troops of horses, the commands of officers or even trumpet calls." Graham, *The Custer Myth*, p. 244.

To get a good feeling of what the men on Reno Hill went through that night, see Willert, *Little Big Horn Diary*, p. 382. "Night of the Besieged" and pp. 385-386 "The Night Between the Battle."

[196]This is a major piece of information on the identification of the bodies on Custer Knoll. All accounts put Lt. Cooke there as well as Chief Trumpeter Henry Voss, but McCarthy of L Company is a new identification.

Charles McCarthy—Private. Born in Philadelphia, Pa. Second enlistment on Sept. 30, 1873, at age 28 in St. Paul, Minn. He had blue eyes, brown hair, dark complexion and was 5' 7" in height. Hammer, *Biographies*, p. 214.

This leaves only one body of the 10 which were found with Custer yet to be identified. Hardorff, *Markers, Artifacts and Indian Testimony* (Short Hills, Don Horn Publications, 1985), p. 4.

Little Bighorn Interviews

Interview with George Gaffney
June 10, 1911, Washington, D.C.

George Gaffney was a Sergeant in I Company. He was born in Cavan, Ireland, in 1846. At the Little Big Horn he was on detached duty in the Quartermaster Department. He had previously served in the Civil War as a member of Company C, 9th Massachusetts Infantry, from 1862 to 1865. He was discharged on Nov. 20, 1881 after his third enlistment, at Fort Totten, Dakota Territory, as a Sergeant of excellent character. He died at the U.S. Soldier's Home in Washington, D.C. on November 22, 1916 and is buried in their cemetery.

He says he was on steamer *Far West* as Assistant Quartermaster with Lt. Nowlan.

He says he cut up teepee poles and made stakes to mark where the officers were buried. One of these was driven into the ground where the body was buried, and each was marked with a Roman numeral burned on with a heated ramrod.[198]

Says Sgt. Varden lay near Keogh.[199]

---

[197]Francis F. Hughes was Private of A Company. Born in Leavenworth, Kansas. Enlisted on May 22, 1875, at age 21 at Fort Lincoln. Previous occupation was laborer. He had blue eyes, brown hair, light complexion and was 5′ 7¾″ in height. Hammer, *Biographies*, p. 212.

In Camp's interview with Roman Rutten, he remembered this about Hughes: "Francis Hughes of Co. L was the last man of the 5 companies coming down Sundance Creek. He had a big black horse which he could not control and he could not ride him in the company and so he followed behind." Camp, *Custer in '76*, p. 120.

Hughes body was identified by Private Foley who claimed he was laying near Custer. Hammer, *Custer in '76*, p. 147. However, McVeigh claims he was laying in a deep ravine (gully) with E Company. Here is another instance where two men were certain they saw the same body in two different places.

[198]We have known stakes were marked by numbers and driven next to the officers' graves, but this is the first time we learn how the numbers were placed on the wooden stakes.

[199]Frank E. Varden. 1st Sergeant I Company. Born in Yarmouth, Maine, second enlistment on May 26, 1872, at age 26 in Shelbyville, Ky. He had blue eyes, brown hair, light complexion and was 5′ 10″ in height. Hammer, *Biographies*, p. 172.

Lt. Edgerly's account of where Varden was found agrees with Gaffney. Edgerly stated: "Sergeant Varden found near Keogh." Hammer, *Custer in '76*, p. 58.

Camp on Custer

His address is: 333 Missouri Ave. N.W. Washington, D.C.

[Camp asked Gaffney] What statement, if any, did Korn make to anyone at Ft. Lincoln after campaign was over about escape from Custer?

He never heard of it.

Was he in the 7th Cavalry in 1866?

Yes. Says he was in the Battle of Washita.

When did Muggins Taylor leave the boat at mouth of the Big Horn?

He does not know.

Interview with John Fox, D Company

John Fox was a private in D Company. He was born Buffalo, New York, on January 3, 1844. He enlisted on September 24, 1875, at age 28 in St. Louis. His previous occupation was cooper. He was discharged on Sept. 23, 1880, at Fort Yates, Dakota Territory, as a Sergeant of good character. He later served in the 1st, 2nd and 4th U.S. Infantries from 1880 to 1897. He died at the U.S. Soldiers Home in Washington, D.C. on December 26, 1932, and was interred on the grounds.

He has discharge papers, signed by Edgerly in 1880, saying that Fox took part in Little Big Horn and Bear's Paw. He says he heard a conversation between Weir and Reno before D Company went out. He says Weir remarked, "Custer must be around here somewhere and we ought to go to him." Reno said "We are surrounded by Indians and we ought to remain here." Weir said, "Well if no one else goes to Custer, I will go." Reno replied, "No you can not go. For if you try to

Little Bighorn Interviews

Captain Thomas B. Weir as he appeared in 1865 as a Major in the 3rd Michigan Cavalry. From a previously unpublished photograph *Courtesy, Chris Kortlander, Custer Battlefield Museum, Inc., Garryowen, Montana*

do it you will get killed and your Company with you." Fox says Reno appeared to be intoxicated or partially so. He says that Moylan and Benteen stood by and heard what Weir said and they did not seem to approve of Weir going and talked as though to discourage him.[200]

---

[200]There are many accounts of what took place on Reno Hill between Weir and Reno before his company moved out. These accounts range anywhere from no confrontation at all, see Bruce R. Liddic's article in *Three Hits and a Miss*, John M Carroll (ed) (Bryan: Privately Printed, 1981), pp. 46-57, to angry retorts and hot exchanges of uncomplimentary language in which threats were made by both parties. Fred Dustin, *The Custer Fight*, (Hollywood: Privately Printed, 1936), pp. 21-22.

According to Fox, Benteen and Moylan heard the conversation between Weir and Reno. However, Benteen in his narrative of the battle claims he never even knew where D Company was and had to inquire of Reno the whereabouts of Captain Weir. Graham, *The Custer Myth*, p. 181. He then changed his story stating, "About this time I saw one of my troops of my battalion proceeding to the front mounted. It was Captain Weir, who sallied out in that direction in a fit of bravado, I think without orders." Charles Kuhlman, *Legend into History* (Fort Collins: Old Army Press, 1977), p. 99.

One guess is as good as another as to what Benteen really saw, heard or did during the campaign.

Camp on Custer

Finally, Weir said that he was going anyhow and Reno did not object. He says Weir went as far toward Custer as any of D Company and when he saw the large number of Indians, ordered the Company to fall back. He says Charley was hit while D Company was falling back and called out that he was hit and implored them not to go off and leave him.[201]

On 6/28 he helped bury the dead on Custer Ridge. The officers were found mainly on the plane and the enlisted men of all 5 companies were mixed up all over the battlefield. He identified enlisted men of 5 Companies and saw this fact of his own knowledge. Says he identified the men of 3 of the companies lying right around Keogh.[202]

In burying the dead, the squad he was in had only one shovel.

They dug up the ground with knives and chopped it with an axe. They threw dirt and sage brush on the bodies. They covered only the faces of some of the bodies.

Edgerly called "Big Feet" says Fox and others.

---

[201] Vincent Charley was Farrier of D Company. Killed in battle at Little Big Horn. Born in Lucerne, Switzerland. Enlisted on March 4, 1871, at age 22 in Chicago. Previous occupation was farmer. Discharged on March 4, 1876, at Ft. Lincoln upon expiration of service as a Farrier. Reenlisted on March 5, 1876, at age 27 at Ft. Lincoln. He had hazel eyes, red hair, sandy complexion and was 5' 10¼" in height. Hammer, *Biographies*, p. 95.

For an account of this action, see Gordon Batemen, "Who was Left to Die at Weir Point," *Little Big Horn Associates Newsletter,* July 1967, Vol. 1, #7.

[202] It would appear from reading these interviews that a great many of the dead on the Custer Battlefield were identified by the burial details. However, only 39 bodies have been accorded with identification today. Hardorff, *The Custer Battle Casualties*, p. 94.

It would be difficult to assess at this late date why the troopers recognized by Fox and others were not better noted and marked on the battlefield

Little Bighorn Interviews

Interview with Sergeant T. W. Harrison of D Company
June 11, 1911[203]

Thomas W. Harrison was a Sergeant in D Company. He was born in Sligo, Ireland, in 1849. He enlisted for a second time on Aug. 10, 1871, at age 22 in Mt. Vernon, Kentucky, and was discharged on Aug. 5, 1876, at camp at the mouth of Rosebud Creek, Montana, as a Sergeant. He died in Philadelphia, Pennsylvania, on December 25, 1917, and was buried in the Holy Cross Cemetery there.

Harrison says the place where Edgerly had trouble mounting his horse was at the north or northeast end of the sugarloaf east of the two peaks. Weir and D Company had stopped back at the south end of this sugarloaf and Edgerly said he would go out to the end of the sugarloaf to look down and see if he could see Custer while they were out there. D Company started back on the retreat. Charley was hit in this retreat back near a ravine to left. Perhaps a ¼ mile or less from the two peaks.[204] As Edgerly and Harrison were coming off the sugarloaf they had to throw their bridles over

---

[203]This interview was in 1911. In a private letter, Camp wrote that he was still trying to prove or discredit Peter Thompson's account: "...Old Sergeant Harrison and Sergt. Bresnahan, whom Gen. Godfrey and I met in 1916, and talked over that whole matter of Weir's advance, were very clear about all details and neither of them saw or heard anything about Thompson." Hammer, *Custer in '76*, pp. 125-126.

[204]The place where Vincent Charley was wounded and later killed was near Weir Point. Weir Point is a group of 3 promontories which resemble a sort of triangle. The base points are along the river's bluffs west of the present road. The peak point lies east of the road and presents, on its eastern most projection, a round sugarloaf appearance which is described by Harrison. Camp noted the distance from South Weir Peak (sugar loaf) to where Charley was hit as 650 feet. The coulee where Charley was killed runs east and west all the way down to Cedar Coulee. Camp goes on further to state A. N. Grover, the second superintendent of the Custer Battlefield found a body in 1903 exactly where Charley had been buried. Hardorff, *The Custer Battle Casualties*, p. 160.

Camp on Custer

Sergeant Thomas W. Harrison, Company D
Courtesy, Little Bighorn Battlefield National Monument

their heads and draw revolvers and ride through the Indians as they came along by Charley. He (Charley) cried out that he was wounded and needed assistance. Edgerly stopped and told him to get into a ravine and he would try to come back and save him as soon as they could get reinforcements. After going a piece they looked back and saw the Indians finishing up Charley.[205] At the moment they were talking with Charley, perhaps 200 Indians were in the immediate neighborhood, all advancing.[206]

He says Weir was with the Company on the peaks and sugarloaf.

---

[205]This is a startling new piece of information. Charley was shot through the hips and when he fell, struck his head and it bled. Charley tried to keep up with the retreating company as best he could, half crawling on his feet and one hand. Hammer, *Custer in '76*, p. 57. Hardorff, *The Custer Battle Casualties*, p. 160.

Little Bighorn Interviews

Interview with Sam Bruguier
February 29, 1912
Regarding the capture of Rain-In-The-Face

Sam Bruguier was a half-breed, the youngest son of Theophile and Dawn (a Santee Sioux) Bruguier. He was born in 1855. In the early 1880s he freighted to Ft. Keogh, Montana, where he served as interpreter. In June of 1881 he and his brother John accompanied the bands of surrendered Sioux who were sent in a fleet of steamboats down to Standing Rock, where he remained as an interpreter. From 1892 to 1909 he was an agency farmer, after which he became a justice of the peace at McLaughlin, South Dakota, where he died in 1929.

Rain-In-The-Face had boasted to several that he helped kill Honsinger and Baliran.[207] Sam and John

---

It was at this point Edgerly and his orderly, Harrison, came upon Charley. Edgerly told Camp he directed Charley to get into a ravine, out of danger for awhile and he (Edgerly) would be back for him with reenforcements. Hammer, *Custer in '76*, p. 57.

Edgerly throughout his life always claimed and even so testified under oath at the Reno Court of Inquiry that he asked Captain Weir for reenforcements to rescue "a man who had been wounded and whom I promised to save." Weir replied, according to Edgerly, "he was sorry but he couldn't stop our movement." Utley (ed.), *The Reno Court of Inquiry*, p. 342.

Harrison's statements to Camp contained in this interview claim both he and Edgerly knew Charley was dead shortly after they left him. Edgerly would have no reason to ask Weir to "save a man" who was already dead. To avoid taking the blame for abandoning a wounded man to hostiles (Charley was later found with a stick rammed down his throat) Edgerly shifted the responsibility for the decision onto Weir at the Reno Court in 1879. This was convenient as Weir died in December 1876 and Harrison was discharged in August of that year. There were many officers of the 7th who wished the entire Weir Point episode would be gone and forgotten. In light of Harrison's statements, this was especially true for Winfield Scott Edgerly.

[206]That the hostiles were advancing on the Company, there can be no doubt. As soon as D left their positions on Weir Point, Edgerly recorded they: "...had closed in on us and were on a knoll less than twenty paces from us, shooting as rapidly as they could." John M Carroll (ed.), *The Gibson and Edgerly Narratives* (Bryan: Privately Printed, n.d.), p. 11. Also refer to Hammer, *Custer in '76*, p. 57.

[207]This was Dr. John Honsinger, the Regimental Veterinarian and Augustus Baliran, the Sutler on the 1873 Yellowstone Expedition. For a detailed account of their killings, see John S. Gray, "Custer Throws a Boomerang," *Montana*, April 1961, vol. 12, #2, pp. 3-4.

Camp on Custer

Bruguier were both at Standing Rock then and heard him telling about it. John Bruguier some time later met Gen. Stanley (By way of verification see what Stanley's command was in 1874—Col. 22 Infantry) and told him of the matter and Stanley said he would order Custer to arrest Rain-In-The-Face.[208] He also wanted to know if John Bruguier would point Rain-In-The-Face out to the soldiers, but Bruguier said he would be in fear of losing his life if he did.

When the soldiers came down looking for Rain-In-The-Face and Brave Bear, John Bruguier was clerking in the trader's store at Standing Rock. This was a long log building. J. R. Casselberry was proprietor of the store.

---

[208] General David Stanley, commander of the Yellowstone Expedition, told a slightly different account of how Bruguier heard of the killings. He reported in the winter of 1873 that John, while attending ceremonies in the Sioux lodges, listened as Rain-In-The-Face made his boast. National Archives, *Records of the War Dept. Letters Received*, 1224-AGO-1874.

Trading Post at Standing Rock Agency where Rain in the Face was arrested by Captain Thomas Custer in 1874. Photo by D.F. Barry, 1880s.
Courtesy, Denver Public Library, Wesern History Department

The soldiers were around the Agency several days but could get no one to identify Rain-In-The-Face. They asked John Bruguier several times to do this and finally he consented to do it in a sly way. One day Rain-In-The-Face and his squaw and several other Indians were in the store, Rain-In-The-Face having a Winchester rifle under his blanket and two six shooters in his belt, Bruguier was clerking and in order to identify Rain-In-The-Face in a way that could not cause suspicion as to who the informant was, he gave Rain-In-The-Face a white shirt with a starched bosom and touched his vanity by telling Rain-In-The-Face that he would look good in it.[209]

Rain-In-The-Face was delighted and put it on and hung around the premises on display. Tom Custer was the officer who had been looking for Rain-In-The-Face for some time and presently he came in and Bruguier told him that the Indian with a new white shirt with the stiff bosom was the right fellow. Tom slipped out and had the soldiers drawn up near the store and then went in with "Isaiah" for an interpreter.[210]

Tom walked up (over) to Rain and shook hands and said "How Kola" and told him he was under arrest. Isaiah was so frightened or disconcerted that he trembled from head to foot and could not get the words out

---

[209] One of the problems the soldiers had in trying to arrest Rain-In-The-Face is no one knew what he looked like. This is the first account of how the soldiers actually identified Rain-In-The-Face, without the Indians knowing who pointed him out. See Captain George Yates' lengthy report of the affair, reprinted in Gray's "Custer Throws A Boomerang," pp. 6-7.

[210] This was Isaiah Dorman. He was later killed in the valley fight. As a civilian black interpreter, he was employed many times by the Army. His last assignment was on the 1876 Campaign. He was formerly a woodcutter for Durfee & Peck and was married to a Santee Sioux woman. He was known to the Indians by the name of "Teat." For a biography of Dorman, see W. Boyes, *Custer's Black White Man* (Washington: South Capital Press, 1972).

of his mouth. Rain-In-The-Face wanted to know what was the matter and Bruguier told him he was under arrest. Rain-In-The-Face submitted quietly and went along. There was no struggle and no grabbing him behind the back, as the story is usually told. The soldiers put Rain-In-The-Face in the corral and left for Ft. Lincoln the next morning before daylight.

Bruguier says the river [Missouri. Ed.]was solidly frozen over and that the soldiers came down on the ice and that they had teams and bobsleds with them. About the next March Rain-In-The-Face escaped and came down and went to the Cheyenne River Reservation to conceal himself.[211] At the time Rain-In-The-Face was captured another Indian named Brave Bear was wanted by the soldiers for killing a family in Minnesota, but they did not get him.[212] He returned in 1877 wearing the clothes of a man known as Johnson whose body had been found with evidence that he had been murdered. He left the reservation again and escaped in 1881. He came down from Canada with Sitting Bull and was tried and hung for his crimes.[213]

---

[211]It has been put forth that to alleviate the embarrassing situation in which the army found itself for holding Rain-In-The-Face for three months without charging him with a crime, it contrived to let him escape. The official story was "grain thieves" who were imprisoned, along with Rain-In-The-Face, were rescued by their friends and out of pure generosity helped the Indian get out of jail as well. Steward, *Custer's Luck*, pp. 59-60. David F. Barry, *Indian Notes on the Custer Battle* (Baltimore: Proof Press, 1939), p. 25.

[212]Brave Bear was also being sought for arrest at the same time. (December 1874) as was Rain-In-The-Face. He was one of the known murderers of the Delorme family on July 5, 1873, near Pembina, N.D. McLaughlin, *My Friend the Indian*, p. 11.

[213]For an account of the killing of Johnson for which Brave Bear was hanged in 1881 at Yankton, Dakota Territory, refer to Ibid., pp. 13-14.

Little Bighorn Interviews

Interview with Sam Bruguier
Regarding the Bozeman fight of April 1874[214]

Near the mouth of Greenleaf Creek the wagons were attacked first by Minneconjous and next reinforced by Hunkpapas. One of the Blackfoot Sioux killed here was Bloody Knife *(Tamila)*. He was brother of Lt. Bullhead who was killed in Sitting Bull's capture on the Lodgegrass Creek fight. They were reinforced by Cheyennes. These Bozeman men were such good marksmen that the Indians could not get anywhere near without getting hit or losing a horse.[215]

They would put up a rag on a ramrod and hold it up and the white men would put a bullet through it.

Bruguier says that there was a tepee or two in the camp of the white men and the Sioux though there must be some Crees among them or some race of fighters superior to the whites.

Gall was in this fight as well as Sitting Bull. The Sioux told Bruguier that these were the hardest fighters they ever ran against on the plains. They appeared to go just where they wanted to and they could get nowhere near them, without losing men or horses.

---

[214] This was the Yellowstone Wagon Road and Prospecting Expedition of March 1874. It was organized and sent out into Indian country to prospect the country between Bozeman and the mouth of the Tongue River on the Yellowstone. Mark Brown, *The Plainsmen of the Yellowstone* (N.Y: G. P. Putnams & Sons, 1961), p. 211. For an excellent overview of the entire expedition see James S. Hutchins, "Poison in the Pemmican," *Montana*, Vol. 8, #3, July 1958, pp. 8-25. In addition, the first full-length treatment of this important journey is covered in Don L. Weibert, *The 1874 Invasion of Montana* (Billings, Mont: Privately Published, 1993).

[215] Brown claims the attack by the Sioux took place on Lodge Grass Creek and involved hundreds of mounted Indians. Brown, *The Plainsmen of the Yellowstone*, p. 217. The 147 men were experienced frontiersmen and prospectors. They were well armed with the latest breech loading rifles with over 40,000 rounds of ammunition as well as two pieces of artillery.

Camp on Custer

They could not get near enough day or night to capture even a horse. Their marksmanship at long range was the best they had ever experienced. They could not understand it except on the theory that some new race of strangers had come into the country.[216]

In one place they found a grave and headstone and a rope. One of the Indians tried to pull the rope up and exploded a bomb. It frightened the Indians terribly but did not hurt any of them seriously.[217] The first fight where the pits are now was about a mile below mouth of Greenleaf Creek.

The Lame Deer fight[218]

He says his brother John had been out to Lame Deer's camp and talked with Lame Deer and had told Lame Deer that if he did not go in to Keogh and surrender by a set time Miles would come out and take him. Lame Deer refused to go in and surrender and Miles kept his word. He says Miles through this trip of Bruguier, knew all the while where the Lame Deer camp was.[219]

---

[216] Sitting Bull, according to Lt. Bradley, declared later that "...he had never seen such men" as the likes of this party of whites. Ibid., p. 213.

[217] For a detailed description of this booby trap and the Indian reaction after it exploded, see Topping, *Chronicles of the Yellowstone*, pp. 116-17. Also refer to Brown, *The Plainsmen of the Yellowstone*, p. 217.

[218] For a good account of this fight, see Jerome A. Greene, "The Lame Deer Fight," *By Valor and Arms*, vol. III, #3, pp. 11-21.

[219] According to Nelson Miles, it was the Cheyenne's White Bull and Brave Wolf and the Minneconjou Sioux Hump who located the Lame Deer Camp. Nelson A. Miles, *Personal Recollections* (N.Y: DaCapo Press, 1969), p. 248. However, George B. Grinnell agrees with Sam Bruguier—these Indians helped Miles locate the camp but Bob Jackson and John Bruguier led them. *The Fighting Cheyennes* (Norman: University of Oklahoma Press, 1966), pp. 393-96.

Interview with A.W. Dale
Regarding the body found on the Rosebud
March 2, 1912

> *Alfred W. Dale was attached to the Medical Department on the 1876 expedition aboard the steamer* Far West. *Dale first enlisted in 1869 under the name Alfred Dormitzer. His fraudulent enlistment was discovered in January 1872 and he was dishonorably discharged. Dale must have enjoyed his life in the Army as he worked to straighten out his past problems and by the end of 1872 was allowed to reenlist as Alfred W. Dale. In February 1876 he was appointed Hospital Steward from his former rank of Sergeant, Company G, 20th Infantry. When Camp interviewed Dale in 1912, Dale was living in Sioux City, Iowa.*

When we marched up the Rosebud, it was a very hot day and I had four ambulances. Two men out on the right flank gave out and I went out with ambulance and picked them up. About this time, some enlisted man who saw we were going out wanted to know whether I was going out to pick up the dead man, explaining upon inquiry by me that a dead man, dead horse and carbine had been found by the Crow scouts out west of the Rosebud. I said I would not go unless I got orders.[220] When I went in, I asked Dr. Williams if he had heard about the matter and he said he had not. That evening, I again asked him if he had heard of the matter and he replied that he had heard of the matter and he seemed to be quite indifferent as though it was of no particular importance. For this reason, I never mentioned the matter to him again. I

---
[220]See Walter Camp's interview with Frank W. Sniffin, herein, for further details on this body found on the Rosebud. Also refer to Robert C. Doran, "The Man Who Got To The Rosebud," *1st Annual Symposium*, June 26, 1987, pp. 19-33.

wrote Dr. Williams' report of the expedition and no mention was made of the matter. In making up this report, we drew largely upon General Terry's records for our data.

My information about the incident at the time was that the horse was a branded sorrel cavalry horse and the opinion was generally expressed to the effect that it must be one of Tom Custer's men escaped from the battle of the Little Big Horn. Although I cannot now be certain, my recollection is that a squad was sent out and buried the body of the man.[221]

I am now (March 2, 1912) certain that Callahan was the nurse detailed with Dr. Lord and Chris Pandtle with Dr. Porter. Hobart Ryder was also detailed as nurse or surgeon's orderly at Powder River on the way out and went with Custer's command. He went down with the wounded on the *Far West*.[222]

---

[221]In these interviews, two constants stand out. One was Camp's efforts to find out the identity of the man discovered on the Rosebud. The other was his attempt to prove or disprove the stories of Peter Thompson and James Watson. Camp went to extraordinary lengths to gather every scrap of information he could find.

[222]John J. Callahan, Corporal, K Company. Killed in battle, June 25. Born in Salem, Mass. Enlisted on November 5, 1872, at age 21 in Boston. Previous occupation was courier. He had gray eyes, dark hair, fair complexion and was 5' 7" in height. Kenneth Hammer, *Biographies*, p. 190.

August Seifert told Camp that Callahan was not with Dr. Lord but was killed when his horse ran away with him as Benteen approached the river. Lt. Godfrey, however, agreed with Dale. Callahan was detailed as acting hospital steward to Dr. Lord. Godfrey was in a position to know—he was Company K's commanding officer. Hardorff, *The Custer Battle Casualties*, p. 111

Christopher Pandtle, Private, E Company. On extra duty as hospital attendant from May 1, 1876. Born in Germany. Enlisted on October 28, 1872, at age 23 in Pittsburgh, PA. Previous occupation was sawyer. Discharged June 10, 1877, at Ft. Abraham Lincoln as a Private of good character. He had brown eyes, light hair, fair complexion and was 5' 4½" in height. Hammer, *Biographies*, p. 116. Hobart Ryder, Private, M Company. Born in New York City. Enlisted on September 15, 1873, at age 27 in Chicago. Previous occupation was broker. On detached service with field hospital with the wagon train. Discharged on September 15, 1878 at Camp Ruhlen, Dakota, upon expiration of service as a Corporal of excellent character. He had gray eyes, dark brown hair, fair complexion and was 5' 7¼" in height. Hammer, *Biographies*, p. 232

Chapter 3

Miscellaneous Notes

March to the Little Bighorn

MARCH TO CROW COUNTRY?

About paying the men after the expedition had got 10 miles out from Ft. A. Lincoln, so that all the money was taken along and there was no chance to spend it.[223]

MARCH TO POWDER RIVER?

Taken from notes on muster roll of A Company, June 30, 1876.

Left Ft. Lincoln May 17 as part of the Big Horn Expedition under the command of Brig. Gen. Terry.

Arr. at Powder River June 11. Left Powder River June 20 arr. at Rosebud June 21.

[Here Camp repeats himself again. "On the march Arr. at Powder River 6/11 Left Powder River June 20. Arr. at Rosebud June 21"].

---

[223]It is a well known fact that the 7th Cavalry was not paid their accumulated three months' wages until they made camp at the Heart River on the afternoon of May 17. Dustin claims Terry was responsible for this order while Charles Windolph stated Custer was. See Fred Dustin, *The Custer Tragedy* (El Segundo: Upton & Sons, 1987), pp. 49-50. Frazier and Robert Hunt, *I Fought With Custer* (N.Y.: Charles Scribner & Sons, 1947), p. 53. Both accounts agree on the reason: to prevent the men from going on a drunken spree prior to the start of a campaign.

Camp on Custer

Private Thomas O'Neill,
Company G
*Courtesy, Little Bighorn
Battlefield National Monument*

INDIAN BURIAL GROUNDS?

Tom O'Neill[224] told me that when the regiment got to the mouth of the Tongue they found a lot of Sioux graves in trees and that some of these were taken down by the soldiers and robbed and thrown into the Yellowstone.[225]

---

[224]Thomas O'Neill was in the valley fight, he joined the Reno Battalion on the hilltop. Born in Dublin, Ireland. Second enlistment in January 17, 1872, at age 27 in Chicago by Captain Samuel Young. He was a cook for Lt. McIntosh in the 1876 Sioux Expedition until June 25. Discharged June 19, 1877, at Fort Lincoln, Dakota, upon expiration of service as a Private of good character. Reenlisted July 15, 1877, at Fort Lincoln, discharged July 14, 1882 at Fort Snelling, Minn., upon expiration of service as a First Sergeant. He had blue eyes, black hair, fair complexion and was 5' 8" in height. Hammer, *Biographies*, p. 147.

[225]Many accounts exist of this grave desecration. In perhaps the best one, Godfrey remarked: "A number of their dead....were disturbed and robbed of their trinkets. Several persons rode about exhibiting the trinkets with as much gusto as if they were trophies of their valor and showed no more concern for their desecration than if they won them in a raffle." Captain Edward S. Godfrey, "Custer's Last Battle," *Century Magazine*, Jan. 1892, vol. 43, p. 362.

Miscellaneous Notes

MARCH TO BATTLEFIELD?[226]

Ragsdale says that when soldiers began to rob Indians' graveyard, the Rees Indians were displeased and Bloody Knife raised objections to the officers and had it stopped.[227] Says that he heard some of the officers express superstition over the desecration of Indian graves.

Regarding the Water Party

John Henley says Thos. W. Coleman was first to run from the gully to the river and bring back water.[228] When Coleman started out he took two camp kettles and said that if he was hit he would call out, and re-

---

[226]John S. Ragsdale was on detached service from June 15, 1876, at Yellowstone Depot, Montana. Born in Hardin County, Ky. He enlisted on July 23, 1872, at age 22 in Elizabethtown, Ky. Previous occupation was farmer. He was discharged on June 24, 1877, at camp on Tongue River, Montana, as a private of good character. He had blue eyes, light hair, fair complexion and was 5' 7" in height. In 1927 he resided at the National Military Home, Dayton, Ohio, and died there on December 4, 1942. Hammer, *Biographies*, p. 54.

If in fact Private Ragsdale was detached on June 15, he could have only been told of this incident by his fellow A Troopers as the graves were not disturbed until the following day. Willert, *Little Big Horn Diary*, pp. 147-148.

[227]For a biography of this famous scout, see Innis, *Bloody Knife*. There is no mention of this incident in the book. As with everything else in the Custer Battle, even this minor point of grave robbing is in dispute. Stewart, among others, claims it was not the soldiers at all, but the Crow Scouts who were taking their vengeance out on the bodies of their hereditary enemies. Edgar I. Stewart, *Custer's Luck* (Norman: University of Oklahoma Press, 1955), p. 231.

[228]John Henley was not at the Little Bighorn. He was a Sergeant of B Troop until his discharge in March 1875. Upon his separation from service James Hill was promoted to this position. It can only be assumed Henley remained in touch with his former B Troopers and from them obtained this account of the Water Party. Hammer, *Custer in '76*, p. 7. A full length biography of Thomas W. Coleman is available. See Bruce R. Liddic, *I Buried Custer* (College Station: Creative Publishing Co., 1979). Coleman makes no mention in his diary of being a member of the Water Party. However, there is little doubt that he was. Stanislaus Roy listed him as a participant and now Henley. If Coleman was the first to the river, he was as deserving of the Medal of Honor as the others of the party who received this award. Hammer, *Custer in '76*, p. 115.

quested that in such case some one run out and relieve him of the kettles. Boren took station near the mouth of the gulley to do this. Coleman made a dash to the water and filled both kettles and got back without being hit. As he approached Boren, the latter held out his hands to relieve him of the load, but Coleman excitedly refused to give them up until he had taken a drink himself first. Other personal remarks spoken through the excitement of the moment occasioned some laughter among the party.

WATER PARTY

Sivertsen[229] says when men went down to bring up Mike Madden,[230] Indians lying on the opposite bank and shooting at them would yell out in good English "Come on over on this side, you Sons of... and we will give it to you! Come over!"

---

[229]John Sivertsen was in the valley fight, was with Lt. DeRudio in the timber. He joined the command later and participated in the hilltop fight. He was born in Norway and enlisted on June 19, 1873, at age 31 at Fort Rice, Dakota Territory. Previous occupation was blacksmith. Discharged on June 19, 1878, at Fort Lincoln, Dakota Territory, upon expiration of service as a private of excellent character. He had blue eyes, sandy hair, light complexion and was 5' 10" in height. He was later retired to the National Soldiers Home, Washington, D.C., and died there on August 30, 1925. Hammer, *Biographies*, p. 233.

[230]Mike Madden was wounded in the right leg in the first water party in the hilltop fight on June 26. Dr. Porter amputated his leg on the battlefield. Promoted to sergeant on June 26, 1876, for his gallantry in the field. Transported to Fort Lincoln on the steamboat *Far West*. Born in Galcony, Ireland. Second enlistment on August 18, 1871, in Louisville, Ky. Discharged at Fort Lincoln on August 28, 1876, upon expiration of service as a sergeant of excellent character. Later employed in the harness depot at the Department of Dakota in St. Paul. Hammer, *Biographies*, pp. 190-191.

There are some who contend white men were with (helping) the Indians at the Little Big Horn. Major Reno thought he was fighting not only all the Sioux nation but every half-breed and squawman west of the Missouri. Stewart, *Custer's Luck*, p. 422. This would account for the "good English" Sivertsen heard coming from the Indian side of the river. However, Col. William Graham did not believe any white men were in the Indian camp. He claimed stories of such were "figments of imagination." William A. Graham, *Story Of The Little Big Horn* (Harrisburg: The Stackpole Co., 1959), pp. 138-39.

Private John Sivertsen,
Company M
*Courtesy, Little Bighorn
Battlefield National Monument*

[Written on the pages of a small diary Camp recorded the following information on the members of the water party. It is believed his informant was Stanislaus Roy.][231]

Water Parties. Afternoon June 26. First Party:

H Troop
    Sharpshooters: Serg. Geo. Geiger
    Blks. Henry W. Mecklin
    Saddler Otto Voit
    Chas. Windolph

A Troop
    Corpl. Stanislaus Roy
    Neil Bancroft
    David W. Harris

B Troop
    Sgt. Rufus D. Hutchinson
    James Pym
    Thos. J. Callan

D Troop
    Chas. H. Welsh
    Abram B. Brant
    Fred K. Deetline
    Wm. M. Harris
    Geo. D. Scott
    Thos. W. Stivers
    Frank Tolan

C Troop
    Peter Thompson

G Troop
    Theo. W. Goldin

---

[231] Stanislaus Roy was in the hilltop fight. Born in France, second enlistment on January 19, 1874, at age 28 in Cincinnati, Ohio. He was awarded the Medal of Honor on October 5, 1878, with the citation "Brought water to the wounded under most galling fire of the enemy and at great danger to his life in the Little Big Horn Fight." Discharged January 18, 1880, at Fort Meade, Dakota, upon expiration of service as a sergeant of excellent character, he re-enlisted in October 1887 as a sergeant in Company A. He had brown hair, brown eyes, light complexion and was 5' 5" in height. Hammer, *Biographies*, p. 48. Camp conducted a rather lengthy interview with Roy on May 2 and again on September 16, 1910. Hammer, *Custer in '76*, pp. 111-18.

Camp on Custer

Water Parties—Other parties who went for water after first party:

Charles Campbell G
John E. Hammon G
Mike Madden K
James S. Tanner M
(afterward killed)

Foley, Rott & Rafter All of K
James M. Rooney F night
of June 25
Frank Hunter F
John Kanagh D

Roy says there were only 12 in the first party instead of 19. He is sure of the names of 9 as follows:

Roy   Golden   Wilber   Voit
Gilbert Bancroft   Peter Thompson
Madden   Harris

Thinks Tanner, Boren and Coleman may be other 3.
[After Camp had compiled this list of names from Roy he apparently tried to organize them into some kind of order to eliminate duplication with other names which had been provided to him. The following is his attempt:]

First Water Party—p.m. 6/26

H Troop
    Sharpshooters: Serg. Geo. Geiger
    Blacksmith Henry W. Mecklin
    Saddler Otto Voit
    Chas. Windolph
Troop A
    Sgt. Stanislaus Roy
    Neil Bancroft
    David W. Harris
Troop B
    Sgt. Rufus Hutchinson
    James Ryan
    Thos. J. Callan
Troop D
    Chas. H. Welsh
    Abram B. Brant
    Frederick Deetline
    Wm. M. Harris
    Geo. Scott
    Thos. W. Stevens
    Frank Tolan

Troop C
    Peter Thompson
Troop G
    Theo. W. Goldin
    Chas. Campbell
    John E. Hammon
Troop K
    Mike Madden
    Foley
    Rott
    Rafter
Troop M
    James Tanner (killed)
Troop I
    James M. Rooney
Troop F
    Frank Hunter

Miscellaneous Notes

[In the same small diary book Camp made a list of questions he wanted to ask at the next interview. These were then crossed out afterwards]

How many Crows corralled with Reno? How dressed? What kind of horses?

    Gerard saw five or six

Did any Crows leave on night of June 25th?

    Gerard says no.

About Boston Custer?

What men of A Troop were left in the timber and came out about 5 or 6 p.m.

    Think there were 2 of them. Ditto G Troop.

Was Sgt. Butler's horse killed with him?

    Martin says yes.

About enlisted men of any troop on Custer Battlefield being identified. Who and where found? Were any of those with Keogh recognized? Sun time & St. Paul time?

Did he see Custer's or Tom Custer's body and those wounded?

Regarding Indian Strength at Little Bighorn

STRENGTH OF INDIAN WARRIORS AT
BATTLE OF LITTLE BIG HORN.

It would seem that part of the 2,000 odd Indians at the Standing Rock Reservation in the summer of 1881 had come from Ft. Keogh as well as from Buford according to the account in Grant Marsh's book p. 412.[232]

---

[232]The book referred to is Joseph Mills Hanson, *The Conquest of the Missouri* (N.Y: Murray Hill Books, 1946).

Camp on Custer

Apparently these included many who had surrendered to armies during some years past. Notice in report of the Com. Indian Affairs 1881 report of the agent at Standing Rock that he gives this number of warriors among there as more than 800.

Get at the Indian population at Little Big Horn by adding together all who surrendered at different times or perhaps better no[.] hostiles reported at Standing Rock in summer of 1881. These were the ones who had surrendered at Ft. Keogh during the several years past and those who had surrendered at Poplar & Ft. Buford in 1880-1881. To these (above 2,800) add those who surrendered with Crazy Horse, the Cheyennes, those with Sitting Bull later, etc. These figures do not include any who may have slipped back to the Agency soon after the battle.[233]

Regarding Bradley's Scout, Little Bat and Crazy Horse

BRADLEY'S SCOUT

Bradley's scout, Wilson, before starting, Capt. Bell tried to swim 17 horses tied together. Had a skiff ahead

---

[233] It would appear Camp was trying to use the census figures and various counts at the Agencies to determine the Indian population at the Little Bighorn. Gray, *Centennial Campaign*, pp. 308-20, had come upon the same idea as Camp had nearly a half century ago in compiling his (Gray's) estimate of Indian strength. For a good summary of all "population accounts" see the extensive footnote 15, p. 309-12 in Stewart's *Custer's Luck*.

[234] For a detailed account of trying to ferry horses and men across the Yellowstone on this 17th of May, see Willert, *Little Big Horn Diary*, pp. 9-14. Another well written account is found in Roger Darling, *A Sad and Terrible Blunder* (Vienna, VA: Potomac Western Press, 1990), pp. 105-123.

Miscellaneous Notes

and one horse tied behind another. These horses were all drowned. Others say only 5 drowned. Sgt. Wilson, steamer *Western*, Capt. McGuire sent Ball, Stewart and Evans across Yellowstone.[234]

LITTLE BAT

Little Bat, a half breed and noted scout, was killed by James Hagnewood in a saloon now in Crawford, Neb., in November 1900. Bat had no weapon at the time and although boisterous while drinking he was known to be harmless.[235]

CRAZY HORSE

Killed Sept. 5, 1877, at Ft. Robinson.[236] On Oct. 27, 4,600 Indians of Red Cloud Agency and Spotted Tail Agency were ordered to the Missouri River to receive winter supplies at the mouth of the Yellow Medicine River on the Missouri. They arrived there in Nov. On this journey the remains of Crazy Horse were taken along says the report of agent James Irwin.

Notice—This was about 75 miles enroute from Red Cloud Agency in Neb. Crazy Horse was buried secretly by his father somewhere in northern Nebraska or southern South Dakota, but, as with Moses, "No man knoweth of his sepulcher unto this day."

---

[235]"Little Bat" was Baptiste Garnier who was employed as a scout for Lt. Col. Carr's 5th Cavalry in the 1876 campaign. See Paul L. Hedren, *First Scalp for Custer* (Glendale: Arthur H. Clark Co., 1980), pp. 37-39.

[236]For an in depth account of the death of Crazy Horse, refer to Robert Clark and Carroll Friswold, *The Killing of Crazy Horse* (Glendale: Arthur H. Clark Co., 1976). The standard biography of this noted warrior, although dated, remains Mari Sandoz, *Crazy Horse, Strange Man of the Oglalas* (N.Y: Alfred Knopf, 1942).

Camp on Custer

Regarding the Death of Spotted Tail

Spotted Tail was born in 1823 on the White River west of the Missouri River in southern South Dakota. His father was a Blackfoot Sioux and his mother a Brulè. Spotted Tail had a keen mind and through his association with the white man at Fort Leavenworth and Fort Kearney he learned as much as he could about the white man's ways. In fact, he was one of the few Brulè who could read and write English. He was recognized as one of the best Brulè leaders by both the Indian and white worlds.

The earliest documented photograph of Spotted Tail, Brulé Sioux Chief. Photo attributed Alexander Gardner before 1868.
Courtesy, Leon Kramer

Miscellaneous Notes

By the late 1860s he became Chief of the Lower Brulès. Spotted Tail, always friendly to the white man, did not join his fellow tribesmen in the 1876 campaign and as a reward the government made him chief of all the Dakota Sioux agencies. In keeping with his peace-making nature, he arranged the surrender of his nephew, Crazy Horse, in 1877.

Spotted Tail was killed near the Rosebud Agency in South Dakota on August 5, 1881, by a fellow tribesman, Crow Dog.

Killed Aug. 5, 1881, by Crow Dog. Spotted Tail had called a council prior to a contemplated visit to Washington. After the council, which broke up at 3 p.m., there was a feast after which Spotted Tail mounted his horse and started home. Crow Dog and his wife were in a wagon approaching Spotted Tail. As Spotted Tail rode up Crow Dog got out of his wagon, stooped down and then suddenly raised up and shot Spotted Tail through left breast. Spotted Tail fell from his horse, but immediately got up and started toward Crow Dog trying to draw his pistol when he reeled backward and fell dead. Crow Dog jumped in his wagon and drove off at full speed toward his camp 9 miles away.[237]

The crime came about partly through an old feud and Crow Dog was supposed to have committed the act at the insistence of Black Crow, one of the head men of the Brulès and a desperate character who wanted Spotted Tail's position as Chief.

---

[237] This account compares favorably, although there are a few discrepancies, with the story told to George E. Hyde, *Spotted Tail's Folk* (Norman: University of Oklahoma Press, 1961) pp. 331-33.

Camp on Custer

White Swan, Crow Scout

White Swan was a Crow Scout. He enlisted in the 7th Infantry for six months on April 10, 1876, at Crow Agency, Montana Territory. He was detached to the 7th Cavalry on June 21, 1876. White Swan accompanied Lt. Charles Varnum on his trip to the Crow's Nest on the morning of June 25th. He was one of ten Indians in the valley fight where he was severely wounded in the right hand and leg after the retreat after crossing the ford. He died on August 12, 1904, at Crow Agency, Montana, and is interred at the Custer Battlefield National Cemetery.

He was wounded in Reno valley fight.

He was deaf and after he was wounded twice, still wanted to stand and fight the Sioux, but Half Yellow Face[238] prevailed upon him to get out of there and he did so and Half Yellow Face led White Swan's horse up the bluffs and White Swan thus rode his own horse up.

Now Half Yellow Face made a travois and took him to the boat. He sat doubled up between the two travois poles just behind the horse and was carried very nicely and many of the soldiers commented on his ingenuity.[239]

---

[238] Half Yellow Face, Private, Crow scout. He enlisted in the 7th Infantry on April 10, 1876, by Lt. James Bradley. He was the leader of the Crow scouts. On detached service from June 21 with 7th Cavalry. Assigned to Major Reno's column. Accompanied Lt. Charles Varnum on the trip to the Crows Nest. One of the ten Indian scouts who participated in the Valley fight; on the skirmish line with the Reno Column. Hammer, *Biographies*, p. 34.

[239] For further details on the Crow scouts and their part in the battle, refer to Graham, *The Custer Myth*, pp. 5-26. Also refer to Camp's interview with August Seifert for additional information on the part White Swan played in the Valley fight.

Miscellaneous Notes

Mark Kellogg, Newspaper Correspondent

Marcus Henry Kellogg was a newspaper correspondent working for the Bismarck Tribune. *He was killed with the Custer column and his body found within "a stone's throw" from the river. Mark was born in Brighton, Canada, on March 31, 1833. He married Martha Robinson on May 19, 1861, and had two daughters. Three of his articles about the expedition were published in the* Tribune.

The New York *Herald* July 11, 1876, page 2 col. 4 contains his notes written up to June 21 and dated mouth of the Rosebud. These are said by *Herald* to be his last written messages.[240]

Biographical sketch N.Y. *Herald* July 10, 1876 col 1, page 23. Here C.D. Smith says his body was found ½ mile in rear of Custer's column. This would likely place him on side hill at marker nearest river as at that time it was supposed Custer had gone that way.

Another account says his body was the last one buried.[241]

Interview With John Burkman

John Burkman was a private in Company C. He was born on January 10, 1839, in Allegheny County, Pennsylvania, although he

---

[240]This last story can be found most conveniently in Graham's *The Custer Myth*, pp. 233-34. For a very good biographical article on Mark Kellogg, see Lewis O. Saum, "Col. Custer's Copperhead: The Mysterious Mark Kellog," *Montana*, vol. 28 #4, October 1990, pp. 12-25.

[241]Camp is correct in his notes as to Kellogg's body. Col. Richard Thompson, Private George Glenn and Lt. Edward Mathey all gave Camp the information recorded here. Hardorff, *The Custer Battle Casualties*, pp. 121-22.

Camp on Custer

later stated it was really in Germany. He first enlisted in the 7th Cavalry in September of 1870. John reenlisted on September 1, 1875, at Fort Abraham Lincoln, Dakota Territory. He was discharged on May 17, 1879, at Fort Lincoln, for disability, as a private of good character. He died of a self-inflicted gunshot wound in Billings, Montana, on November 6, 1925, and is interred in the Custer Battlefield Cemetery.

Custer had two horses, Dandy and Vic. The latter he rode on the day of the battle. He was a Kentucky horse, sorrel, with three white stockings and a white face. Early in the day he rode Dandy, but changed and took Vic.[242]

Was E or L companies on Reno's scout and any circumstances he remembers.

Burkman says L troop was there.

How come Jasper Marshall to be at Powder River wounded on June 30, 1876?[243]

Does not know. He was wounded on Reno Hill in the heel with two bullets in the same wound.

---

[242] Complete details of Vic, Dandy, and the rest of Custer's horses can be found in Lawrence A. Frost, *General Custer's Thoroughbreds* (Mattituck: J.M. Carroll & Co, 1986).

[243] Jasper Marshall, Private, L Company. With the pack train detail on June 25. Wounded in the left foot in the hilltop fight on June 26. Transported to Fort Lincoln on the steamer *Far West*. Born in Ohio, enlisted on September 22, 1875, at age 22. Previous occupation was farmer. Discharged on February 9, 1877, at Ft. Lincoln for disability as a Private. He had gray eyes, black hair, dark complexion and was 5' 5½" in height. Hammer, *Biographies*, p. 213.

Chapter 4
Indian Interviews

Interview with Thomas Disputed
Regarding the Battle of Little Bighorn and action at Medicine Tail Ford

THOMAS DISPUTED
(A Kinichaki)
Ogallala under Big Road[244]

The Blackfeet were with the Hunkpapas and not by themselves. Minneconjou next, Sans Arc next, Cheyennes next, Ogallalas and Brulès together over toward hills. Each formed part of the circle. Santees next north of Cheyennes. Only a few Santees there under Inkpaduta. Ogallalas had fewer than Hunk or Minneconjou.[245]

When Reno appeared the Indians were not prepared and went over to the hills to consider, and after some firing, decided to fight them and did so and chased them out of the valley.[246]

---

[244]Big Road was an Ogallala warrior chief who fought Reno in the Valley. Hyde, *Red Cloud's Folk*, p. 268.

[245]There has always been different interpretations of just where each camp circle was located. One of the best descriptions is by Wooden Leg. Thomas B. Marquis, *A Warrior Who Fought Custer* (Minneapolis: The Midwest Co., 1931), p. 387. This agrees closely with Disputed's recollections. For a slightly different arrangement see Hyde, *Red Cloud's Folk*, p. 207.

[246]That the Indians were unprepared at the time of Reno's attack has been well documented by the testimony of the village inhabitants. Thomas Disputed adds the same conclusions to his recollections.
It is interesting to note the differences in how the Indians perceived Reno's assault and

Camp on Custer

I did not get with the Reno Fight, being after my horse, but after it was over bands of Indians had crossed the river and were gathering around on the east side (probably going over to that side) I and another rode up Medicine Tail coulee and started east (parallel with river) toward Reno Hill and discovered soldiers coming down the ravine.[247]

I rode back the way I came and crossed to the village and rode along the river upstream shouting that more soldiers were coming and we would have to have another battle. All along the river there were many dismounted Indians and the banks were steep everywhere except at Medicine Tail coulee. The soldiers came down this coulee toward the river and stopped just a little while, but not long and the Indians crossed over and attacked them. There were a few soldiers ahead of the main body.[248]

There was then firing on both sides and we chased the soldiers up a long, gradual slope or hill in a direc-

---

the view taken by the soldiers. Their testimony and recollections claim the Indians were well prepared and in fact had set a trap for them. Many references and primary sources could be referred to, but they are neatly summarized in Willert, *Little Big Horn Diary*, pp. 283-285.

[247] Apparently Disputed crossed the Little Bighorn River in the Medicine Tail Ford area and turned southeast, but before he could make a flanking move against Reno, he saw more soldiers coming down the coulee. This agrees with John Stand-In-Timber who stated Custer came toward the village from the high ridge to the east. W. Boyes (ed), *Cheyenne Tribal Historian John Stands-In-Timber's Account of the Custer Battle*, (n.p., Little Big Horn Associates, Inc., 1991) p. 2.

[248] This is a valuable account of the fighting at the Medicine Tail Ford. A number of Indian accounts claim there was no fighting there. Those who so claimed probably arrived late from upstream and simply missed seeing the action at the Ford. Jerome Greene, *Evidence and the Custer Enigma* (Golden: Outbooks, Inc., 1986), p. 25. Here we have the Disputed interview, a hostile who crossed the river before the Indians knew there were other troops besides Reno's. He saw the troops, re-crossed the river to warn the others, went back across and saw the action. This should help to put to rest the theories that Custer's troops did not fight at the Ford. As White Man Runs Him stated: "I know for sure Custer went right to the river bank. I saw him go that far." Graham, *The Custer Myth*, p. 15

Indian Interviews

tion away from the river and over the ridge where the battle began in good earnest. The soldiers kept running as if in part of a circle and the last of them had turned to run toward the river again, when all were killed.[249]

We did not suspect that we were fighting Custer and did not recognize him either alive or dead. The horse with a white face and four white feet, which we afterwards learned was Custer's, was caught by a Santee girl and kept by a short man of the Santee tribe.[250] I remember one of our men getting a pearl handle pistol which we afterwards learned had been carried by Custer.[251]

I heard about the soldier who tried to get away on a horse, and shot himself with his pistol and killed him-

---

[249]This account is similar to the ones related to Grinnell in that soldiers crossed a deep gulch and climbed the hill on the other side. Grinnell, *The Fighting Cheyennes*, p. 351. Disputed's account probably describes the action of Companies E and F as they moved from the engagement at the Ford to the high ground north of Deep Coulee. Hardoff, *Markers, Artifacts and Indian Testimony*, p. 39. From here the action became fierce around Calhoun Hill.

Disputed's telling of soldiers at the end of the battle breaking for the river agrees with the book by Gray, *Custer's Last Campaign*, pp. 383-99. Also see Chief Gall's account of these soldiers who fled to the river. Barry, *Indian Notes on Custer's Last Battle*, p. 27.

[250]There are many stories as to what happened to "Vic," the horse Custer rode on June 25. Lt. Edgerly claims he saw Vic dead on the battlefield. Hammer, *Custer in '76*, p. 58. Lt. McClernand also saw a dead horse on the field which was pointed out to him as belonging to Custer. E. S. McClernand, "The Fight on Custer Hill," *Cavalry Journal*, Jan. 1927, Vol. #36. Col. Homer Wheeler stated in 1877 how he visited the battlefield and cut the hoofs off the horse that was ridden by Custer. H. W. Wheeler, *Buffalo Days* (Indianapolis, Bobbs-Merrill Co., 1925) p. 184.

These recollections not withstanding, it is entirely possible that Custer's horse was captured as related by Thomas Disputed. Dr. Frost investigated all the various accounts and was not able to reach a definite conclusion on whether Vic was killed or captured. Frost, *General Custer's Thoroughbreds*, pp. 229-244.

[251]Lt. Godfrey remembered that Custer carried 2 Bulldog, self-cocking English, white-handled pistols. For a complete summary of Custer's personal weapons see John S. DuMont, *Custer's Battle Guns* (Canaan, NH: Phoenix Pub., 1988), pp. 61-78.

self.²⁵² The talk among us at the time was that one of the pursuers probably hit him and he, seeing that he could not hold out, decided to kill himself while he still had the strength so as not to fall into our hands alive.²⁵³

The winter before the Custer fight, we had wintered (Ogallalas) on the Tongue. The camp attacked by soldiers on the Powder 3/17/76 was not an Ogallala camp and Crazy Horse was not there, because I was with Crazy Horse all the while.²⁵⁴

I was in the fight on the Rosebud 8 days before the Little Big Horn. It has been a matter of debate with us whether this fight took place 8 or 9 days before the Little Big Horn.²⁵⁵ At the time we fought Crook, we were camped on a dry stream with some water holes, which rises in the direction of the Rosebud and flows into the Little Big Horn. We were near some pine

---

²⁵²Two Moon and Wooden Leg also told about the soldier with braid on his arms who crossed a ditch and went over a ridge before he shot himself. Thomas B. Marquis, *A Warrior Who Fought Custer* (Lincoln: University of Nebraska Press, 1965), p. 232. Graham, *The Custer Myth*, p. 103. Hardoff, among others, claims the trooper was Corporal John Foley of C Company. Hardoff, *Markers, Artifacts....*, p. 60. In addition, the Cheyennes told Grinnell an account similar to the one related by Disputed, see Grinnell, *The Fighting Cheyennes*, p. 353.

²⁵³The Cheyennes had told Dr. Marquis that there was no reason for the whites to believe that the Indians wanted to take them for torture and that there "is no rational ground for a supposition such as this." Thomas B. Marquis, *Keep the Last Bullet For Yourself* (N.Y: Two Continents Pub., 1976), p. 71. However, after reading what he told Camp, Disputed knew why Foley committed suicide "so as not to fall into our hands alive." This agrees with the conclusions reached by Dr. Holmes Paulding who was with Terry's column. Dean Hudnutt, "New Light on the Little Big Horn," *Field Artillery Journal*, July-August 1936, vol. 26, #4, p. 349.

²⁵⁴The best book on the Powder River fight is J. W. Vaughn, *The Reynolds Campaign on the Powder River* (Norman: University of Oklahoma Press, 1961). In addition, an enjoyable booklet by Fred Werner, *The Soldiers Are Coming* (Greeley: Werner Pub., 1982) should be consulted.

²⁵⁵The Battle of the Rosebud took place on June 17, 1876. The most recent account of this action is Neil Mangum, *Battle of the Rosebud* (El Segundo: Upton & Sons, 1987).

bluffs.[256] Only part of our men went out to fight Crook. The remainder were left to guard the villages in the direction of the Yellowstone.

We fought the soldiers on the Rosebud and they quit and went back up that stream and out of the country. We did not pursue because we were not particularly anxious to fight if the soldiers would leave us alone.[257]

We had to move camp to the Little Big Horn two days before the battle and did not think the soldiers would come that far to fight us, but when we saw them coming onto us by surprise, we said "There is no use in running from here.[258] We might as well fight right here. If the soldiers have come this far to fight us, they will do it again and they will be bothering our village all the time unless we fight and defeat them."[259]

At time of the fight my name was Shave Elk—Eccoca Taskla, which means "an elk with bare skin in spots."

---

[256] At this time, the combined villages of the Sioux and the Cheyenne had been camped for the past five nights at the forks of Reno Creek. The camp was about two miles in length and centered about where the present road crosses a bridge at its forks. Stewart, *Custer's Luck*, p. 200.

[257] Most Indian accounts agree the hostiles wanted nothing more than to be left alone and follow their old way of life. Sitting Bull is reported to have said we are like "a bird when on a nest spreads its wings to cover the nest and eggs and protect them. It cannot use its wings for defense but it can cackle and try to drive away the enemy. We are here to protect our wives and children, and we must not let the soldiers get them." Dr. Joseph K. Dixon, *The Vanishing Race* (N.Y: Bonanza Books, 1975), p. 174.

[258] Actually the Indians did not move their camp until the 24th. They moved eight miles down to the Little Bighorn. It was at this location that the battle took place the following day. Gray, *Centennial Campaign*, p. 327.

[259] Sitting Bull advised his people in much the same manner: "Warriors, we have everything to fight for, and if we are defeated we shall have nothing to live for." Eastman, "Story of the Little Big Horn," p. 357. Incredibly, John Stands-In-Timber was told by the Cheyennes who were present in the camp that the Indians decided not to start anything, but if the soldiers came to talk to them, if they were peaceable, to find out what they wanted. Stands-In-Timber, *Cheyenne Memories*, p. 192.

Camp on Custer

At the time Crazy Horse surrendered, an officer whom we called White Cap came out and met us and it was arranged to have some of our men meet some of the principal men of the soldiers.[260] When Crazy Horse met White Hat, Crazy Horse said, "All right, I will surrender and fight no more. He then put his head-dress on White Hat and White Hat rode off wearing this headgear and he looked so comical that even we Indians laughed.

Crazy Horse heard that he was wanted at the post (Camp Robinson) to go to Washington, but he would not go, but ran over to Spotted Tail. I was then in the service of the government as a scout and was one of the policeman who escorted Crazy Horse over to Red Cloud.[261]

When we got over there an officer took Crazy Horse by one hand and Little Big Man *(Wicharta Taukala)* by the other and led him off. I had turned to look the other way when I heard Crazy Horse say, "So you intend to put me in the guard house, do you" and he turned to run back. A soldier stabbed him with a bayonet in the right side, the bayonet going nearly through him. (Crazy Horse was stabbed through the kidneys). About this time and while he was struggling to get away from Little Big Man, he drew a knife and cut Little Big Man on the wrist and also in the side

---

[260] "White Cap (Hat)" was Lt. William P. Clark. He was one of the better known officers on the Plains. He graduated from West Point in 1868 and was assigned to the 2nd Cavalry. He came to Gen. George Crook's attention during the Sioux War and was invited to his staff. His service was so outstanding that Gen. Sheridan asked him to be on his staff, but the thirty-nine old officer died suddenly in Washington on Sept. 22, 1884, of peritonitis. *Army and Navy Register*, October 18, 1884.

[261] For the details of these events, see Camp's interview with Louis Bordeaux, July 6 and 7, 1910.

Indian Interviews

under his left arm. This struggle was the end of Crazy Horse.[262]

Chips was a medicine man for Ogallalas, O.K. says Disputed. Toukcha Hausha was a medicine man, but does not remember whether or not he was with Crazy Horse at Little Big Horn.

Thomas Disputed says that about as soon as he began to pursue Custer, his (Disputed) horse was shot and he took it afoot and followed on after the soldiers. He recalls that the soldiers were chased up a long slope or easy hill for the reason that he remembers how tired he became before he got up there.[263]

Interview with One Feather
August 10, 1911

One Feather was an Arikara Indian Scout. He was born in 1831. One Feather's first enlistment was at Fort Lincoln, Dakota Territory, on May 9, 1876. He went on the Powder River scouting trip with Young Hawk on June 10. He was with the Reno Battalion on the afternoon of June 25. After crossing the Little Bighorn he turned to the right to capture a herd of Sioux ponies and drove them across the river to the ridge top. He returned to Yellowstone Depot. He was a brother of Good Elk.

On the night of June 24, we cooked up meat to go out ahead. Red Star came back with a note from Crows Nest. Rees up on Crows Nest.

---

[262]The account of Disputed's involvement with the final days of Crazy Horse agrees closely with others who were there. In particular refer to Robert A. Clark and Carroll Friswold, *The Killing of Chief Crazy Horse*.

[263]Anyone who has walked from the Medicine Tail Ford area across Deep Coulee and up the slopes to Calhoun Hill on a hot June afternoon knows exactly what Thomas Disputed experienced.

Camp on Custer

There were two others but can't remember them[264] (Forked Horn, Red Star) (The Whole Buffalo).

Red Star and Strikes Two helped cut out horses. They took horses back to the hills and went back toward the Sioux with Custer. On the way to the river we found a tepee with dead Sioux. As we neared the river we could see Sioux driving their horses.[265]

Gerard told me to go ahead and if not, he would take our arms away from us. Custer had wanted to know what the scouts were doing and if they were not going to do anything, he would take their guns away from them.

I scolded Gerard for not staying with us so as to give us the orders. Gerard left the scouts and went back with the soldiers and left us without an interpreter.[266]

When close to the village we saw dust rising up high in the middle of the village and the Sioux started toward us and the scouts were half way between the soldiers and the Sioux.

Bloody Knife brought me 3 horses and said take them and if I (Bloody Knife) get through, I want one and you take the other two. There were 3 horses captured from the Sioux. After fuss with Rees Bobtail

---

[264] For Red Star's narrative of these events, see Graham, *The Custer Myth*, pp. 31-33. Forked Horn and Young Hawk's stories continue on pages 34-38.

[265] It was these Sioux moving away from the soldiers which led Custer to commit his forces earlier than he had wished. He thought the village was fleeing and needed to bring them to bay. Willert, *Little Big Horn Diary*, p. 271.

[266] All accounts agree that Custer wanted the scouts to chase after the fleeing Sioux, but they refused to do so. Stewart, among others, claimed the Rees refused to go because of cowardice. One Feather's account relates for the first time why they did not pursue the hostiles, there was no interpreter to tell them what the white man wanted. Fred Gerard, it would seem, was not paying attention to his duty as an interpreter. One wonders what would have been the outcome of the battle if the scouts had ridden after the Sioux and Custer did not order Reno to "charge after them." Stewart, *Custer's Luck*, p. 325. Also, Willert, *Little Big Horn Diary*, p. 271.

Indian Interviews

Bull, Bloody Knife, Forked Horn and *Watokeh* led out and we followed.[267]

I did not take the 3 horses from Bloody Knife. I had a good horse myself. I stood by while white fight going on. I saw 3 Sioux squaws coming behind us and they went into the woods and hid. Went up with scouts with horses and I called on Strikes Two to say what we were going to do with the horses, and Strikes Two made no reply. I saw two other horses and started to get them. I went into the woods and saw a horse of Whole Buffalo and said to him, "What are you doing here. You had better go along and help get horses away." The Sioux fired on men getting away with the horses and wounded my horse in the foot.[268] I tried to save him and other scouts advised me to let him go.

Whole Buffalo, Little Crow (Rushing Bull), Horn-in-Front and others gathered together on the right while the Sioux were chasing us. We were hungry on the way, very hungry, and when we stopped one night we proposed to kill Rushing Bull's colt (Rushing Bull had a mare and a colt).[269] We began begging Rushing Bull and Rushing Bull then wanted to know what it

---

[267]This account by One Feather agreed with Red Bear's. He related how Bloody Knife had gotten three horses from near the Hunkpapa camp. Bloody Knife then called out to Red Bear, "Someone take these horses back to the hill. One of them is for me." Innis, *Bloody Knife*, p. 137.

[268]One Feather's horse was wounded in a fight over the captured horses by the ford. Red Star told how they headed the horses into a group. One Feather had a bunch nearer the ford and these horses were retaken by the Sioux who had crossed the river lower down. Graham, *The Custer Myth*, p. 39.

[269]Rushing Bull was an Arikara Indian scout enlisted at age 45 on May 9, 1876, in the 7th Cavalry for six months. He was on the expedition on June 25, but did not cross the Little Bighorn River into the Valley fight. Joined the six scouts on the ridge top who had captured the Sioux ponies and performed duty as pony herder. Returned to Yellowstone Depot. Discharged at Ft. Lincoln in Nov. 1876 upon expiration of service with good character reference. His age then was 45 and he was 5' 9" in height. Hammer, *Biographies*, pp. 37-38.

was all about and what we wanted, and when we told him, he consented to have the colt killed. And so we killed it and ate it. This colt was following the mare Rushing Bull was riding. Next day we arrived at Powder River camp. Some of us had extra horses on the trip back to the Powder.

I had to change horses on the way back, my horse being wounded and swollen. I got an extra horse from one of the scouts (Foolish Bear). I had to leave my horse there and the next day went back to get him and found him dead. He died with saddle and bridle on (He said this positively, but afterwards corrected himself and said that he took the saddle and bridle off and carried them along).

Foolish Bear gave me the horse (instead of Rushing Bull)[270] on the way, but when we got to the Powder River Rushing Bull gave me a horse and I paid him $10 and I gave Foolish Bear's horse up to him.

When got to the Powder, Whole Buffalo had 2 horses.

Came right back to Powder on the same trail we went to the Little Big Horn.

---

[270] Foolish Bear carried dispatches in the field June 27. He was an Arikara Indian scout. Discharged from enlistment on Jan. 13, 1876. Sixth enlistment at age 28 in the 7th Cavalry for six months on May 9, 1876, at Ft. Lincoln. He carried mail from the Turkey Buzzard Camp (#8) to Ft. Lincoln with One Horn and then returned to the expedition. He carried mail from Rosebud Creek to Yellowstone Depot on June 22. Sick at Yellowstone Depot on June 25. Hammer, *Biographies*, p. 32.

Indian Interviews

Little Bighorn Indian Scouts, 1911 Interviews

REES, MANDANS, GROS VENTRE IN 1873

Crow Breast was Chief of Gros Ventre. Son of the Star was Chief of Rees. Bad Gun was Chief of Mandans. Son of Star's picture is in Taylor's book, *Frontier and Indian Life*.[271] Gerard's picture is in the same book.

Young Hawk
Black Calf
One Feather
Strikes Two
Little Sioux (living)
Soldier (living)
Forked Horn (dead)
Bobtail Bull
Little Brave
Stab (dead)
Bull in Water (dead)
Rushing Bull (dead) (Little Crow—name changed)
Good Face (dead)
Foolish Bear (Foolish Red Bear) (dead)
Strikes the Lodge (dead)
Goose (dead)
Round Wooden Cloud
Bear Come Out
Bear in Timber
White Cloud
Bloody Knife
Black Fox (dead)
Bull (dead)
Bush (dead) (Red Wolf)
Good Calf (Red Bear) (living)
Strike Bear
White Eagle (dead)
William Cross
William Jackson
William Baker

Revised August 10, 1911 Absentees at Little Big Horn. Sent back with messages.

Barking Wolf (dead)
Howling Wolf (dead)
Wolf Runs (Running ?)
Bear (correct name Foolish Bear)
Bear's Eyes (dead)
Long Bear (dead)
Black Porcupine (dead)
Climbs the Bluff (dead) (This man's name was "Wolf")
Curly Head (dead)
Horn in front (dead) (Young Hawk's father)
One Horn (dead)
Laying Down (dead)
Owl (dead)
Wagon (dead)

---

[271] This was a book written by Joseph H. Taylor titled *Frontier and Indian Life and Kaleidoscopic Lives*. It was printed in California in 1902. It is interesting to compare this list of scouts to the names in Hammer, *Biographies*, pp. 27-41. Not only are the scouts names listed, but also a good, concise biography of each.

Camp on Custer

Discharged, not on expedition.

Whistling Bear
Broken Penis
Cards
Left Hand

Sticking Out (see if he was not a Sioux; was not Ree)
The Shield
Robert Jackson

Photograph in *Kaleidoscopic Lives* page 173.

Left to right:

Bloody Knife
Bobtail Bull

Yellow Wolf
Strikes Two (probably)

Killed at or near Ft. Lincoln: Red Bear (father of present Red Bear)

Father of present Boy Chief. Widow now draws pension
Boy Chief (brother of present Boy Chief)
Crow Tail
Stands Among Them
Turkey Buzzard

Chapter 5

The Death of Crazy Horse

Louis Bordeaux on The Death of Crazy Horse
July 1912, Crow Butte, Nebraska

> Louis Bordeaux was a half-breed, the son of James Bordeaux, a trader from St. Louis and his Brulè Sioux wife. The elder Bordeaux had set up a trading post near Fort Laramie, Wyoming, in the early 1840s. Louis's uncle was the Brulè chief Swift Bear. Louis was born in 1850. His father later sent him to Hamburg, Iowa, to be educated. He was the official interpreter at Spotted Tail Agency in the 1870s and thus in an excellent position to participate in the events which occurred there.

Bordeaux says the fight at Crow Butte happened in 1849.[272] The year he was born. His father was a trader who first discovered that Crows were in the country. That night old man Bordeaux sent his Mother (Louise) and children to warn the Sioux, which they did. He pursued them and wounded the Crows up there. Another part of the Crows over on Lover's Leap signaled with mirrors that there were too many Sioux and dare not try to assist. That night the Crows led horses down the rocky gully to the west and escaped.

---

[272]Crow Butte is located on the White River about eight miles east of Camp Robinson, Neb. In the winter count of Iron Shell the year 1849 was recorded as the "Crows Held Sioux at Bay." During the year a war party of Brulès were cornered in a bank by the Crows. Also refer to Garrick Mallery, *Picture Writing of the American Indians* (Bureau of American Ethnology, *Annual Report*, 1888), p. 323.

Touch the Clouds, Minneconjou Sioux Chief
Courtesy, William Eloe

Two Strikes was one of the Sioux there and was wounded.[273]

The Crows were chased up onto the Butte and surrounded. There were only part of the Crows in the vicinity.

---

[273]Two Strikes was a famous Brulè Sioux warrior. He was born in 1821 and had two sons and two daughters. He died in 1914. Hyde, *Spotted Tail's Folk*, p.39.

The Death of Crazy Horse

Lt. William Philo Clark,
2nd Cavalry
*Courtesy, Denver Public Library,
Western History Department*

Touch Cloud and High Bear heard this interview of Crazy Horse with Gen. Bradley which Frank Grouard misinterpreted.

Lt. Clark cried when he heard that Crazy Horse was dead. He said, "It is too bad. That man ought not have been killed. It is a shame the way he was treated."

"Waposta Sha" was White Hat's name.

He says father of Crazy Horse was Crazy Horse. At the time Frank and I disputed about the interpretation, Frank said to me: "Louis you do not understand the dialect of those Northern Indians." And I told him: "Frank you cannot teach me my mother tongue."

135

Camp on Custer

Mr. J. J. Baesle, farmer at Allen, says Tour Todd was the man who stabbed Crazy Horse.[274]

He says Capt. Kennington had the point of his sword against Crazy Horse's body and was yelling "Shoot him! Shoot him!"[275] Baesle says he saw these things. He says American Horse, Red Cloud and the prominent men of the Ogallalas were jealous of Crazy Horse. Crazy Horse was wounded fighting Pawnees instead of Shoshoni, says Red Willow. Bob Waln made a mistake in interpretation. He was shot at the side of his nose by No Water, the bullet coming out the back of his head.[276]

Crazy Horse was buried by Chips and old man Crazy Horse while the Sioux were on the way to Whitestone on the Missouri.[277]

Frank Grouard, the day Crazy Horse was stabbed, came along on a horse and said, "Get on behind me Louis and lets get out of here and go where there are more soldiers. There is going to be trouble, etc."[278]

---

[274] Tour Todd is an entirely new candidate for the soldier who killed Crazy Horse. Most accounts have the dubious distinction belonging to William Gentles. Private, Co. F, 14th Infantry. This private was on sentry duty the afternoon of September 5th at Post #1 near the guard house. As such, it is almost certain he stabbed Crazy Horse during the melee. For a biography of Gentles, refer to John M. Carroll, "The Man Who Killed Crazy Horse," *Old West*, Summer 1991, vol. 27, #4, pp. 38-41.

[275] This account of Captain Kennington's actions during the struggle with Crazy Horse is similar to the one repeated in Stanley Vestal, *Warpath and Council Fire* (N.Y: Random House, 1948) p. 271.

[276] For a good over-view of the ongoing feud between Crazy Horse and No Water over No Water's wife, see Stephen E. Ambrose, *Crazy Horse and Custer* (N.Y: Doubleday & Co., 1975), pp. 311-15.

[277] Chips was indeed the Indian who accompanied Crazy Horse's father to the unknown burial site. The story of how Chips helped the elder Crazy Horse is contained in "Interview with Chips," Feb. 14, 1907, *Richer Tablet #18*, Nebraska Historical Society.

[278] Grouard was not the only one who sensed trouble. Bordeaux knew it was coming as well. In fact, he said quietly to Lee "We better get out of here, if they try to put him in the guard house, there will be a fight and we will get killed for bringing him over here." Clark and Friswold, *The Killing of Chief Crazy Horse*, p. 124.

The Death of Crazy Horse

Bordeaux says there was another camp of soldiers over near the grove.

Frank had a letter from Beaver, his mother was in Beaver, Utah, and from his father in Chicago and his brother used the name Pratt.

Frank had killed a school mate in Ft. Pierre, ran away and went among the hostile Indians.[279]

Walker says Geo. Sword, now dead, was one of the Indians who went out to Crazy Horse's camp and persuaded him to come in during early spring of 1877.[280]

Philo Clark was called "White Hat."

Interview with Louis Bordeaux on the Death of Crazy Horse
July 6 and 7, 1910 Valentine, Neb.

In the late winter or early spring of 1877 Spotted Tail went out to the hostile camp of Crazy Horse to talk peace and try to induce the Indians to come in and surrender.[281] He talked with the principal men and they agreed to his proposals. Crazy Horse was not in the village, his being encamped some distance away, but the prospects were so honorable for the surrender of the whole band that he sent word to Crazy Horse

---

[279]The complete details of Frank Grouard's family and the various names associated with the members is contained in John S. Gray, "Frank Grouard: Kanaka Scout or Mulatto Renegade?" Chicago Westerners *Brand Book*, Oct. 1959, Vol. 16, #8. The above account also contains the details of Grouard's involvement in the death of his classmate.

[280]The story of how Red Cloud's nephew, (George) Sword, first led a party of Ogallalas in the winter of 1877 to Crazy Horse's Camp to urge them to give up and come into the agencies is contained in Hyde's, *Spotted Tail's Folk*, p. 267.

[281]General George Crook had persuaded Spotted Tail to go out to the hostile camps and make peace. Spotted Tail was a shrewd negotiator and from the General obtained very liberal peace terms. On Feb. 15, 1877, accompanied by 250 Brulè warriors he left his agency and started for the hostile camps. Hyde, *Spotted Tail's Folk*, p. 264.

Camp on Custer

Red Cloud, Ogallala Sioux Chief, as he appeared for the camera of Alexander Gardner, 1872, in Washington, D.C. *Courtesy, Paul Harbaugh Collection*

representing on what terms he could surrender and then returned to the Agency at Camp Sheridan. The communication reached Crazy Horse who sent word to Spotted Tail that he would come in and surrender. After a little while Crazy Horse and his band came in and put up their lodges on Hat Creek and Lt. Clark (Philo Clark) and Garnett[282] went out and talked with him and he went in to the Red Cloud Agency and surrendered, instead of coming to Spotted Tail where

---

[282]William Garnett was born in 1855 at Ft. Laramie. His mother was Sioux, his father Major Richard Garnett. The older Garnett would later become a general in the Confederate service and fall in Pickett's Charge at Gettysburg. William lived with his mother's people and became an expert scout and interpreter. He knew just about everyone—red and white—in the Fort Robinson area. Clark and Friswold, *The Killing of Chief Crazy Horse*, pp. 73-74.

The Death of Crazy Horse

Spotted Tail expected him to come and where if he had come there would have been no further trouble.[283]

While Crazy Horse was at Red Cloud there was a scout who had been with Gen. Crook the year before named Ephraim Pratt (Prigo?) commonly known as Frank Grouard.[284] Grouard had been with Crazy

---

[283] This is at variance with what Spotted Tail told Lt. Jesse M. Lee. Upon his return from the hostile camps on April 5, he reported Crazy Horse would surrender at the Red Cloud Agency. Red Cloud was not only Crazy Horse's uncle, but an Ogallala as well. General Crook, anxious to hasten the surrender, sent Red Cloud out to move the hostiles along. On May 5 Crazy Horse arrived at his Ogallala uncle's Agency and surrendered in the presence of Crook and his officers. Hyde, *Spotted Tail's Folk*, p. 269. Also see Sandoz, *Crazy Horse*, pp. 360-62.

[284] Frank Grouard, by all accounts, seems to have been one of the major, if not the major villain in this tragedy.

Frank Grouard, standing at center (and mislabeled "Frank Gerard" on the original glass plate negative), as an interpreter at Pine Ridge Agency at the time of the Wounded Knee Tragedy, 1891. Attributed to C.C. Morledge.
Courtesy, Chris Kortlander, Custer Battlefield Museum, Inc., Garryowen, Montana

Camp on Custer

Horse about 5 years as a hostile and after Crazy Horse surrendered Grouard became afraid and very fearful of Crazy Horse and thought that Crazy Horse might seek occasion to take revenge on him for destroying the Indians' homes with the Army the year before.[285] When he saw that everything had settled down to a peaceful basis he thought that by stirring up trouble Crazy Horse might be disposed of in some manner that would remove him as a standing menace to himself.[286] Accordingly, Grouard began to circulate stories to the effect that Crazy Horse was becoming discontented and trying to stir up another war.

On one occasion Crazy Horse had a council with Gen. Bradley the commander at Camp Robinson.[287] It was desired that Crazy Horse go out as a scout to help fight the Nez Percé, but Crazy Horse refused. Grouard, who was doing the interpreting, reported Crazy Horse as saying that if the white man wanted any more blood he would propose to take his Indians out and fight it out with the soldiers until one side or the other was exterminated. Grouard reported other things of a boastful or threatening character. Repre-

---

[285] Grouard led Col. J. J. Reynolds' soldiers in a March 1876 attack on the Powder River. See Vaughn, *The Reynolds Campaign on the Power River*.

[286] Mari Sandoz goes further, she claims that Big Bat Pourier said Grouard was sick with venereal disease and he became very dissipated, a physical wreck from hanging around the forts. Mrs. Susan Bettelyoun, Bordeaux's sister, stated that Grouard was afraid when Crazy Horse surrendered and left the Agency. He came back, gave false interpretations and lied to get Crazy Horse, who knew about his past, out of the way. Sandoz, *Crazy Horse*, p. 426.

[287] Camp Robinson was the site of the Red Cloud Agency. It was located on the headwaters of the White River in northwestern Nebraska. Lt. Col. Luther P. Bradley was second in command of the 27th Infantry. This was the same Luther Bradley who commanded Fort C. F. Smith at the time of the Hayfield Fight in 1867. His action, or rather lack of it, in going to the rescue of this group of soldiers is still debated. Jerome A. Greene, "The Hayfield Fight," *Montana*, Oct. 1972, vol. 22, #4, pp. 30-43.

Bradley was born in 1822 in Connecticut and held the brevet of Brigadier General for the battle of Resaca. He retired in 1886 as Colonel of the 13th Infantry.

The Death of Crazy Horse

Fort Robinson, Nebraska, as it appeared at the time of Crazy Horse's death. Photo by C.C. McBride. *Courtesy, Paul Harbaugh Collection*

senting that he was quoting Crazy Horse, whereas Crazy Horse was ignorant all the time of what was going on and did not understand what all the trouble was about.[288]

Finally, the government ordered that Crazy Horse be arrested and taken to Camp Robinson which was

---

[288]There is little doubt that Grouard was responsible for the deliberate mistranslations of Crazy Horse's words.

Toward the end of August, Lt. Clark was ordered to recruit a group of scouts among the Sioux to aid him in the capture of the Nez Percé. The council was held at Red Cloud Agency. *South Dakota Historical Collections*, vol. 17, p. 315. Due to this twisting of Crazy Horse's words, the recruitment of Sioux was canceled and the military was ordered to keep a close watch on the Northern Sioux to prevent a breakout and alliance with the Nez Percé.

Clark relates how only Bordeaux was aware of what Grouard had done and the two exchanged angry words over it. Clark and Friswold, *The Killing of Chief Crazy Horse*, pp. 29-30.

It should be noted that in Joseph DeBarthe's book, *The Life and Adventures of Frank Grouard* (Norman: University of Oklahoma Press, 1958) there is no mention of this episode. However it is too well documented not to have occurred. The eye-witness account by Bordeaux solidifies this viewpoint.

141

Camp on Custer

located where the post is now and about three miles from Red Cloud. Crazy Horse got information of this and slipped away and went over to Camp Sheridan to Spotted Tail Agency, where I was the official interpreter. Here he was met by Spotted Tail, Lt. Jesse M. Lee, Maj. Burke and others and Spotted Tail addressing Crazy Horse spoke frankly to the following effect,[289] "Crazy Horse, you have come into a peaceable community. My Indians are at peace with the government and we are on amicable terms with the authorities at Washington, and by being reasonable we can get what we want. If you can come with us and do like we do and be quiet and peaceable we will be glad to have you with us. If not, we had rather you would not come, as we desire to keep out of trouble."[290]

Not being well acquainted with Crazy Horse I was surprised at his reply and the intelligence which he displayed. He was evidently not a talkative man, but on the occasion he made quite a long speech and his remarks showed him to be a silent man of careful thought and good judgment, and accustomed to councils on important affairs, a man of more than ordinary mental ability.[291] He began by saying that over at Red

---

[289] Captain Daniel W. Burke was the commander of Camp Sheridan which was located at the Spotted Tail Agency about 40 miles downstream from the Red Cloud Agency. 1st Lt. Jesse M. Lee was the adjutant of the 9th Infantry. This was the same Lt. Lee who 18 months later would be the recorder in the Reno Court of Inquiry. Thomas Bookwalter, *Honor Tarnished* (n.p: Little Horn Press, 1979), pp. 4-5.

[290] Hyde states this council was held in the evening of September 3rd at the commandant's office at Camp Sheridan. Crazy Horse had already agreed to go back to Camp Robinson with Lt. Lee. The purpose of the council was to get Crazy Horse away from the Spotted Tail Agency without angering the Sioux and bringing on a fight. Hyde, *Spotted Tail's Folk*, p. 284.

[291] This is the standard interpretation of Crazy Horse's character. He was an individual who made a distinct impression on all who came in contact with him. Bordeaux was no exception.

The Death of Crazy Horse

Cloud there were bad winds blowing. He did not understand why it was so but that there was feeling against him there, and he was being misrepresented. He was desirous of having peace, for which purpose he had surrendered and he would be glad to do anything to keep out of trouble, but he did not think this would be possible over at Red Cloud. He would therefore like to be transferred to Spotted Tail Agency where things were quiet and no winds blowing. He would be out of the turmoil and he would assure them that if this request would be granted they would find him a peaceable Indian.[292]

All these things I interpreted to Lt. Lee and Maj.

---

[292]Hyde states that Crazy Horse did not want to be a peaceable Indian. He was planning to break away with his camp and return to the Bighorn Country, thus breaking his pledge to Crook that he would remain quietly at Red Cloud Agency. George Hyde, *A Sioux Chronicle* (Norman: University of Oklahoma Press, 1980), pp. 4-5. Also see Hyde, *Red Cloud's Folk*, pp. 295-96.

Trading Post at the Red Cloud Agency
Courtesy, Wyoming Historical Society

Burke. These officers were then instructed to how the reported threats and conspiracies of Crazy Horse had become current and asked him if he had said such things in council as Grouard had reported him to have said. All those things Crazy Horse denied, saying that Grouard had entirely misquoted and misrepresented him. He said emphatically that his every effort had been to promote the peace and if any other opinion of him was entertained then his language had been badly misconstrued. He seemed to be considerably agitated and apprehensive that he had been misrepresented.[293]

His remarks impressed me well and this I say with full knowledge of the Indian character, being born and raised among them and having lived with them all my life, being half Indian myself with a large acquaintance among both Agency Indians and the hostiles. He also made a good impression on Lee and Burke who said they would take my interpretations in preference to those of Grouard.[294]

On one occasion I had been interpreter at a council where Grouard was present and he disputed the accuracy of my interpretations, saying that the hostile talked differently from the Brulès and other Agency Indians, among whom I had lived. Now Grouard was a very ignorant man in the use of English and his Sioux speech was very broken, so I told him openly in council that he must have nerve to try to teach me my

---

[293] Not only was Crazy Horse, according to Bordeaux, agitated and upset, he was also portrayed as having fearful premonitions. Clark and Friswold, *The Killing of Chief Crazy Horse*, p. 34.

[294] Hyde defended Grouard saying, "There seems to be very little truth in these stories" that Grouard misinterpreted Crazy Horse's words. Hyde, *Red Cloud's Folk*, p. 295. This is definitely a minority viewpoint. In particular refer to a scathing indictment of Grouard in Julia B. McGillycuddy, *McGillycuddy Agent* (Stanford: Stanford University Press, 1941), p. 65. The vast amount of evidence supports the deliberate misinterpretation position.

The Death of Crazy Horse

mother tongue, and that a man of his limited knowledge should be ashamed of making the pretension of which he was guilty. I say these things to show that the confidence of the officers at Camp Sheridan in Grouard's knowledge of Sioux and his reliability in general were not by this time well established, and they accepted Crazy Horse's statements of his case.

It was now told to Crazy Horse that he had been ordered brought to Robinson and the only thing for him to do was to go over there and make his statement of his case there. He was under some misgivings and did not know under the circumstances what was best to do. If Lee and Burke would promise to intercede for him with Gen. Bradley and have him transferred to Spotted Tail, he would go.[295] This they promised to do saying they would do all they could for him and Crazy Horse promised to go and asked for something to eat.

Crazy Horse was then handed over to Touch Cloud, a Minneconjou and told he would be responsible to see that Crazy Horse did not get away. Crazy Horse went with Touch Cloud and the next morning early we started for Robinson, Lee and myself riding in an ambulance drawn by four mules and Crazy Horse riding his own horse right behind the ambulance and escorted by a considerable party of Indian Police from our own Agency which was augmented until we had about 60 of them before we got to Robinson.[296] We

---

[295] The account of Crazy Horse asking Lee to intercede for him is in line with all the other accounts, before Bordeaux's became known. Clark and Friswold, *The Killing of Chief Crazy Horse*, pp. 34-35. Vestal, *Warpath and Council Fire*, pp. 269-270. Sandoz, *Crazy Horse*, pp. 402-403.

[296] This account is very similar to the one Lt. Clark gave in his report to the Commission of Indian Affairs, Sept. 10, 1877, NARS, R.G. 75, Spotted Tail Agency.

Camp on Custer

did not stop at Red Cloud but went right on into Camp Robinson. The adjutant quarters were in a new building, and as we rode up, Lt. Lee, our acting agent, had a talk with Gen. Bradley, and then came to me and said: "The plans we had in view to try to get Crazy Horse transferred over to our Agency have fallen through. The matter is in the hands of my superior officers and I can do nothing. They have made arrangements to take him to Ft. Laramie and perhaps elsewhere and get him away from here. Do not tell him about this, for if they try to put him in the guard house there will be trouble with all the Indians around here. Let us keep out of the squabble. We have brought him over here and done our duty to the government and done all we could for him, so lets not say anything that will stir up trouble."[297]

We had expected that Crazy Horse would be permitted to make an explanation and request to be transferred to our Agency, but Gen. Bradley would not hear of this and acted in every way arbitrarily. Lee now went to several of the principal chiefs standing around to watch what was going on, including Big Road, Touch Cloud, Standing Bear and others and said wearily that the officers would take care of Crazy Horse to which they all replied "all right."

When Crazy Horse dismounted Little Big Man ran up to him in a rather superior manner and as though he was running the business, and grabbed him by the

---

[297]William Garnett's account at this point makes no mention of Lt. Lee interceding for Crazy Horse. He said Crazy Horse arrived at about 3 o'clock on Sept. 5 and was immediately taken to the guard house. Clark and Friswold, *The Killing of Chief Crazy Horse*, pp. 84-93. Also see the account by Red Feather in John M. Carroll, *The Eleanor H. Hinman Interviews* (n.p: Garry Owen Press, 1976), pp. 34-35. Red Feather agrees with Garnett.

The Death of Crazy Horse

sleeve and said: "Come on you coward."[298] At this Crazy Horse seemed much astonished, but said nothing, evidently not knowing what to think of Little Big Man, who at one time had been one of his intimate friends. At length the Officer of the Day came along and walked up to Crazy Horse and said: "Come with me," motioning to him,[299] where upon Little Big Man again became assertive of authority and pulled on Crazy Horse's arm, and said again "Come on you coward." Crazy Horse walked along between them, evidently not suspecting where they were intending to take him until he walked past a guard into the guard house.[300] Suddenly realizing where he was, he turned and started to run back where upon Little Big Man grabbed him by the arm and tried to pull him back. At that, Crazy Horse quickly drew a knife and cut Little Big Man on the wrist. There was a struggle between the two and a large man who stood guard, wearing a red beard, gave Crazy Horse a heavy thrust with his bayonet in the right side, the bayonet piercing the kidney and going nearly through him—so near that the

---

[298] All accounts agree Little Big Man played the part of the troublemaker throughout this whole sad affair. See in particular Sandoz, *Crazy Horse*, pp. 406-408; and Vestal, *Warpath and Council Fire*, pp. 271-272.

[299] The officer of the day was Captain James Kennington of the 14th Infantry. Clark and Friswold, *The Killing of Chief Crazy Horse*, pp. 124-126.

[300] Major Thomas Tobey's account claims the army was only going to keep Crazy Horse in the guard house temporarily, but not as a prisoner, to keep him out of harm's way. Carroll, "The Man Who Killed Crazy Horse."

However, the Major's story is probably a cover-up as Bradley stated his orders from Crook were to send Crazy Horse to Omaha. Crook, strangely enough, notified General Philip Sheridan that Bradley was sending him to Cheyenne, Wyo. James C. Olson, *Red Cloud and the Sioux Problem* (Lincoln: University of Nebraska Press, 1975), p. 244. To further complicate the matter, Lt. Lee heard from a second-hand source that Crazy Horse's eventual destination was to be Dry Tortugas, Fla. E. A. Brininstool, *Crazy Horse* (Los Angeles: Wetzel Pub. Co., 1949), p. 34.

Camp on Custer

Little Big Man from a previously unpublished carte de visite, ca 1875. *Courtesy, Paul Harbaugh Collection*

skin on his left side became puffed out and swollen.[301] Crazy Horse had on only leggings and his waist and back were bare. The guard quickly jerked out the bayo-

---

[301]There are a number of accounts which are at variance with Bordeaux's remembrances. Little Big Man, no doubt to deflect criticism of himself for the role he played, claimed Crazy Horse stabbed himself with his own knife after Little Big Man tried to prevent Crazy Horse from hurting anyone. Hyde, *Red Cloud's Folk*, pp. 297-98. Little Big Man told a similar story to Bourke. John G. Bourke, *On The Border With Crook* (N.Y: Scribner's & Sons, 1891), p. 422.

There is no doubt, however, that the bayonet was the death instrument. Dr. Valentine McGillycuddy, the doctor who examined Crazy Horse, stated specifically it was an army bayonet. McGillycuddy, *McGillycuddy Agent*, p. 92.

Perhaps one of the most fantastic tales was again related by Major Tobey. He stated that when Crazy Horse saw the bars on the guard house and realizing where he was being taken, rushed out of the building and "impinging upon the bayonet of No. 1 sentinel, who had instinctively lowered his piece to the charge upon hearing disturbance." Carroll, "The Man Who Killed Crazy Horse," p. 41.

The Death of Crazy Horse

net and made another heavy lunge with it, this time missing Crazy Horse and the bayonet sticking fast in the door post. A number of Crazy Horse's friends—one of whom was Touch Cloud and another, my uncle Swift Bear—now ran in and seized him in an effort to stop the scrimmage. Little Big Man getting away. In jerking the bayonet out of the door post the butt of the guard's gun hit one of these friendly Indians in the neck and broke his collar bone. In the meantime, the Officer of the Day became excited and was running about crying: "Kill the son of a bitch! Kill the son of a bitch!" At the same time he was trying to get at Crazy Horse with his sword.

The Indians had gotten around Crazy Horse so thickly by this time that he could not reach Crazy Horse and Crazy Horse who was still on his feet backed up and finally fell.[302] As soon as he fell, one of the friendly Indians ran up and took his revolver which had been on his person and which he had not tried to use. All of this happened very quickly and just about sundown.

Crazy Horse was carried into a building and lived until midnight.[303] His father and mother heard of what had happened and came over to see him. I was there when they entered the room. Addressing him the

---

[302] One of the first to reach Crazy Horse was Dr. McGillycuddy. He had been standing about 25 feet away during the fight. When he wedged his way in past the guards and milling Indians, the doctor "...found Crazy Horse on his back, grinding his teeth and frothing at the mouth, blood trickling from a bayonet wound above the hip." Clark and Friswold, *The Killing of Chief Crazy Horse*, p. 125. William Garnett, another witness, related the following additional details about the wound, "...the bayonet went through both kidneys and within one-half inch of going through the body." P. E. Byrne, *Soldiers of the Plains* (N.Y: Minton, Balch & Co., 1926), p. 240.

[303] After considerable confusion, Dr. McGillycuddy had the soldiers carry Crazy Horse to the adjutant's office. There he was cared for by the doctor until he died. Sandoz, *Crazy Horse*, pp. 409-11.

father said, "Well, my son, how is it with you?" Crazy Horse answered and said "you have come to see me, but you must not have further expectations; I am going to die." At this his mother began to weep.

I talked with Crazy Horse about what had happened, and he said: "The soldiers should not have stabbed me. I had no desire to do injury to any of them. Had I so desired I could have killed some of them, for I had my revolver, but did not try to use it. The only man to whom I wished to do harm was Little Big Man, for his insolent treatment of me, but he got away. I don't know why they stabbed me."

About midnight it was reported to me that Crazy Horse was dead and before daylight Lt. Clark, who had goodwill toward Crazy Horse, came along and inquired about Crazy Horse and I told him Crazy Horse was dead, whereupon he said, "Can it be possible that my friend Crazy Horse is dead, I cannot believe it and then he sat down, hid his face in his hands and wept."[304]

The next day Crazy Horse's parents took his body over to a hill back of the gully, wrapped it in scarlet cloth, such as they had for making leggings, and put it on a scaffold, after the ordinary manner of Sioux burial.

Late in the fall the Indians were moved over to the Missouri River and the body was taken along. On the way, the father and one other Indian took it one dark night and, making a side trip, buried it in the ground, a place unknown to any but themselves.[305]

---

[304] For a different interpretation of Lt. Clark's relationship with Crazy Horse, see Clark and Friswold, *The Killing of Chief Crazy Horse*, pp. 137-39.

[305] Black Elk said his (Crazy Horse) parents hid the body somewhere on Pepper Creek. John G. Neihardt, *Black Elk Speaks* (N.Y: William Morrow & Co., 1932), p. 149. John Carroll summarizes the various accounts of his burial on page 13 in his *Hinman Interviews on Crazy Horse*.

The Death of Crazy Horse

Crazy Horse's name was *Tasunke Witko* which literally means "His Foolish Horse," and the meaning of which is a horse which will rush headlong into battle—one that cannot be restrained. The word *Witko* conveys the thought of foolhardy as impetuous rather than the word foolish in its ordinary sense.[306]

He was of medium height and slim. His features were light and his hair light, being peculiar in this respect. He was a man of mild manners, mild in speech and of gentle disposition.[307] He was a man of ordinary appearance and his presence would not attract notice, either favorable or unfavorable among the Indians. He had a great reputation for bravery and military sagacity, he having become prominent through his many battles with the Crows before he ever fought the white man.

When he died he was about my own age, which was 29. I would not have estimated his age at more than 32, at the most. Among the Indians, his youth was remarkable in such a great warrior.[308]

---

[306] There are as many stories about how Crazy Horse got his name as there are Indians to relate them. But most are in agreement that his name was given to him by his father who possessed that name until he gave it to his son. Afterwards the elder Crazy Horse was known as "Worm." Carroll, *Hinman Interviews*, pp. 12-13.

[307] If one looks closely at the photograph of the Indian opposite page 132 in Vaughn, *With Crook at the Rosebud* it is a remarkable resemblance to this description. Friswold believed the picture to be authentic and wrote a rather detailed account of its history. Clark and Friswold, *The Killing of Chief Crazy Horse*, pp. 45-47. Carroll also gives his opinion on photographs of Crazy Horse. Refer to Carroll, *The Hinman Interviews*, pp. 15-16.

[308] Lt. John Bourke, Crook's adjutant, agreed totally with Bordeaux's assessment: "I have never heard an Indian mention his name save in terms of respect." Bourke, *On The Border With Crook*, p. 414.

Chapter 6

Francis Johnson Kennedy and the Battle of the Little Bighorn

Preface to Statement of Kennedy

Francis Johnson Kennedy was a private in Company I. He was born in Pacific, Missouri, on May 12, 1854. Francis enlisted on September 27, 1875, in St. Louis under an alias—Francis Johnson. His previous occupation was laborer. He was discharged on September 26, 1880, at Camp Houston, Dakota Territory, upon expiration of service as a private of excellent character. Francis died January 9, 1924, and was buried in Calvary Cemetery in St. Paul, Minnesota. It should be noted that on his death certificate, his birthplace was listed as Ireland and his birth date as May 14, 1859, which, as he related, accounted for the use of another name at his enlistment.

Along with a continuing effort trying to establish the veracity of Thompson's account and the identity of the soldier's body found on the Rosebud, the horse Comanche occupied a great deal of Camp's time. He was fascinated, as have been countless other students of the Battle, by the horse. This may account for Camp's inclusion of Kennedy's statement which he copied directly from the archives of the Minnesota Historical Society.

There is no record of Camp ever having personally interviewed Kennedy. His reasons as to why not, when he knew where Kennedy lived, are impossible to know. Camp's goal was to acquire as much information as he could through interviews, letters and previously written reminiscences for his projected book on the In-

Camp on Custer

dian Wars. This account fit his goal since it contained, for the time, a credible narrative about the famous horse.

This statement of Francis Johnson Kennedy was given to Olin N. Wheeler about the year 1900. Mr. Kennedy at that time was a resident of St. Paul, Minnesota. His account was printed in the Minnesota History Bulletin, *Vol. 3, 1919-1920.* John Carroll reprinted parts of it in his "Seventh Cavalry Scrapbook" series, Volume I, in 1978.

Francis Kennedy's reminiscences of twenty-four years past contain a number of statements which are at variance with the known facts. However, his account of finding Comanche is of great interest, especially the statement that Comanche did not go back with the wounded on the Far West. Most other accounts have the horse being put aboard with the wounded. Dr. Elizabeth Lawrence in her brilliant book on Comanche, His Very Silence Speaks, casts doubt on these stories. "It seems remarkable that such great importance was placed upon a lone cavalry horse." In light of what Kennedy remembered, her suspicions have merit.

Not only is there uncertainty as to how or when Comanche reached Fort Lincoln, but the number of his "finders" comes very close to exceeding the number of "survivors" of the Last Stand. To this growing legion of Comanche "finders," we can add the name of Francis Kennedy.

To get an idea of the number of people who claim they were the person who found/rescued the horse, one does not have to research deeply. Their stories have been recounted for better than one hundred years in the literature of the Custer fight, most of which have been neatly summarized in Dr. Lawrence's book on the famous horse. Edgar Stewart also goes into detail on this subject in Custer's Luck.

Another interesting point which Kennedy makes concerns Rain-In-The-Face. Rain-In-The-Face had told Dr. Charles Eastman of a soldier who had befriended him while he was in the guardhouse at Fort Lincoln. Lt. Colonel Custer had ordered his arrest and confinement for the killing of two white men during the Yel-

Statement of Francis Johnson Kennedy

lowstone Expedition of 1873. Up to now, this sympathetic trooper had remained unidentified. Kennedy claims it was Corporal John Wild of his company.

Statement of Francis Johnson Kennedy

Formerly of Troop I, 7th U.S. Cavalry. My full name is Francis Johnson Kennedy, but when I went into the Company, I did not give my full name as I was too young and I went by the name of Francis Johnson.

I was bitten by a rattlesnake at the second crossing of Snake Creek in the Badlands before getting to the Little Missouri. After that, I was detailed to travel to the Powder River and when we got to the Powder River, a company was sent from that point to the Yellowstone River to see if the boat was there and to get supplies. Troop I, to which I belonged, was detached under Captain Keogh for that purpose. There was then detailed five troops for a ten days scout. I would not be positive as to the other companies, but I Troop was one of them under Major Reno. They were to locate any trails of Indians. We traveled up the Powder River and found some Indian trails, getting the main Indian trail at the Rosebud, about 15 or 20 miles from the mouth. We were obliged to turn back from this point, not being strong enough to tackle the Indians, although it was pretty hard to pursuade Reno to do so. We marched down the Rosebud River to the Yellowstone where we met the rest of the command and also General Terry. As we returned from Reno's scout, we joined the main command, near as I can tell, just about where Fort Keogh now stands, about two miles from the present Miles City.

After they got into camp, the officers called the other

Camp on Custer

commanders together to decide what to do. Custer took twelve companies of the 7th Cavalry and took them on the south side of the Yellowstone River, while Terry took the other companies and went around to the other side. Five men were detailed as packers under the citizens, of which I was one.

We started from there and took up the trail we found on the scout and followed it, I think it was for two days (and then made a night march), marching that day until nearly dark and went into camp about four o'clock. I think it was on the evening of the 24th that we found the trail hot and made a night march.

We marched until nearly morning and then lay down by the horses, they being saddled and bridled. We did not build any fires. We took up the trail after getting rested, and the call to halt was sounded just before the officers got ready to charge, but what time it was I do not exactly know. After we started out, I Troop was rear guard and I was leading Keogh's (second) horse, Comanche. This was on the morning of the 25th, I think, and after marching some time there was an officer's call sounded to water the horses at the spring. After officer's call, we marched. Custer took his five companies marching to jump the Indians in three places. Custer took I Troop, E Troop, F Troop, C Troop and L Troop; Reno took three companies in his command and Major Benteen took three companies, B Troop being detached as rear guard in place of L Troop. The officers at this time got orders to bunch the mules together, with the exception of the ammunition mules, which were taken on ahead and then Custer, Reno and Benteen charged in three different directions on the Indian camp. Custer took the end farthest to the right, Reno the center of the main village and Benteen the left end. We followed up Reno's trail with the pack mules, and by the time

Statement of Francis Johnson Kennedy

I got up to the place where Reno went into the fight, they were retreating and had re-crossed the river.

After making the high ground and getting back onto the high bluffs, Reno sent D Troop to reinforce Custer. In my estimation they did not go farther than 500 yards from where we were when they had to turn back to where Reno was stationed on the bluffs, the pack train and Benteen and the rear guard getting up about this time (sometime early in the afternoon, I should say it was). We got out on the skirmish line after the Indians who came down at us all the afternoon until sundown. Then the officers got together and posted sentries or pickets around our line and those who were not detached in this way tried to get what sleep they could until morning.

In the morning, about seven o'clock, the men wanted water. Benteen came around about that time and stated that he had had water at four o'clock that morning. When the boys heard him say he had had water, they said they would get water too and he told them to get what camp kettles or water bottles and canteens they could find and go up to where his company was on the firing line.

When they got there, they were to make a charge and yell for all they were worth, and when they got about 50 yards from where his line was, they would find a ravine. We went down the ravine to the Little Bighorn River and got the water, one of the troopers whose name I think was Mike Madden being wounded in the leg.

In the afternoon of the 26th, about 3:30, I noticed the teepees in the village disappearing. In a short while they were all down. The firing commenced to let up a little and then we saw a body of Indians traveling up the Little Bighorn Valley. We thought they were going to flank us and we entrenched ourselves as well as we could, none of the men having knives, tin cups, etc. with which to dig. We saw no more of them

Camp on Custer

Comanche, Captain Keogh's horse. Photo by D.F. Barry, ca. 1882.
Courtesy, Denver Public Library, Western History Department

after that, but kept watch for them. On the morning of the 27th, we looked for them but could not see anything. After getting breakfast, a man named Ramsey and I, both of us belonging to I troop, started out on our horses to cross the river and see what we could see. We were down there about twenty minutes when recall sounded. While we were coming back, we saw a heavy dust to the right, only further on from the river, made by Terry and his command, and when they came up to where we were, that was the first we knew that Custer had been massacred, Terry coming right from the

Statement of Francis Johnson Kennedy

Custer Battlefield right up the line of bluffs on the east side of the river.

After Terry got in, Ramsey and I went down on the bottom lands and found some of the men that were killed with Reno, stripped and cut to pieces. Among the number was a Negro scout, Isaiah, who was all cut up. Ramsey and I went down in the valley to where there was a teepee still standing in which there were some seven or eight dead Indians. After leaving the teepees, we went still further down the valley. I saw a horse standing there and said to Ramsey that it was Comanche. When we got up there, he was not able to move. He was standing still and had, I should guess, about twenty wounds, some flesh wounds and some more serious. I went hunting around and finally found a camp kettle and went down to the river to get some water, taking some into my hands and washing out his wounds the best I could. We got him down to the river and after getting him there, we met a corporal of the 7th Cavalry and he was detailed to shoot all of the wounded animals. Corporal Reynolds was his name. I asked him to let Comanche stand still until I could get an order from Reno not to have Comanche shot. I got this order and brought him down the river toward our camp, to almost fifty yards of the ford. We left Comanche then with the other horses on the west side of the river and then went back up to where Custer was killed, to help bury the dead. Sometime in the afternoon the 7th Infantry came across and carried our wounded to the other side. In order to carry the wounded, we made travois and had the 7th Infantry lead the mules. We brought Comanche along with the wounded and got him to the mouth of the Little Big Horn River. There was no room for him on the boat with the wounded. It took us a long while to get Comanche along for he was so badly wounded that he

Camp on Custer

had to walk slowly. He was wounded through the front legs and wounded in the neck, also in the hips.

After leaving Comanche and going on the Custer Battlefield, we found that the Details had buried the bodies of the dead. We came up the ravine and walked up to where Keogh was killed. Nolan took the bark off some willow branches and inserted in the hollow bark a piece of paper with the name of the officer written on it and stuck the bark into the head of the grave. When we got up on the ridge, we asked where I Troop was and went on where the troop was. When we got there, we were asked if we could identify any of the men, but all we could identify were two—one of these a corporal named Wild and the other a musician. The way we did this was because the corporal was the biggest and the musician the smallest man. We also identified Keogh. The corporal was uninjured (not mutilated) because he had been kind to Rain-In-The-Face when he was in the Guard House, giving him tobacco, etc. I understood that Rain-In-The-Face said if he had not been killed outright, he would have left him near us where we could have taken care of him. Keogh was not mutilated because he had a gold crucifix hanging about his neck, and Custer was left untouched on account of his great bravery.

The men were cut on all sides and legs, and some were disemboweled and others had their legs taken off. Reno's men were mutilated more than Custer's men. Their faces were decayed and discolored, and some had their eyes dug out, while all had not a stitch of clothes on. Reno's men were scalped more than any of the other men. One dead Indian was found there and some of our men wanted to take his whole head off. He had some gunshot wounds as though someone had fired a shotgun at him.

The men that were with Custer were stripped of all their

Statement of Francis Johnson Kennedy

Captain Myles W. Keogh, Company I. Taken one year before his death at the Little Bighorn. Photo by O.S. Goff, July 1875. *Paul Harbaugh Collection*

clothing after they were killed and cut to pieces, the horses lay cut to pieces also, and we found a man (Hodgson) belonging to G Company lying dead at the brink of the river.

Benteen was talking and encouraging the men on the 25th and 26th, giving them all the encouragement possible. He said "don't you even flinch when you hear bullets go by, for if you do, you will get it in the head for sure." Lieutenants Edgerly, Hare, and Wallace were very brave in the fight. The horses were arranged in a semi-circle with their saddles and bridles on, the wounded being in the valley in between the horses, and any man who went by that horse was sure to be shot, for the horse enabled the Indians to get a good aim at that man. A man was stationed near there to keep the others from passing so the Indians could not get a range on them.

Captain Moylan was not seen from the time the fight on the bluffs started until after it finished. All the dead Indians we saw were then in the teepee. We saw but eight or nine

Camp on Custer

dead Indians on the right hand side of the river. The Crow scouts, Yellow Face and Half-Yellow-Face, I think their names were, were with us in the fight and I believe one of them was wounded in the hand.

Comanche got to Lincoln in pretty fair shape and an order was sent from Washington that he should never be ridden again and in all future ceremonies, he was to be led in front of the Battalion draped in mourning.

Chapter 7

Interview with Luther H. North
April 21, 1917

Regarding the Battle of Summit Springs

Luther North was born in Richland County, Ohio, on March 6, 1846, one of five children of Thomas and Jane Townley North. He, along with his famous older brother Frank, was active with their Pawnee Battalion throughout the Great Plains from 1864 to 1877. The brothers were especially involved with the 1869 campaign, the Black Hills Expedition of 1874 and the Powder River Campaign of 1876. After the passing of the frontier era, Luther was occupied in farming and cattle ranching and until 1890 lived in the Black Hills country of South Dakota. He moved to Omaha and in 1898 married Elvira S. Coolidge. He worked for the Internal Revenue Service and they remained in that city until 1917 when they returned to Columbus, Nebraska, where Luther died on April 17, 1935. They had no children.

Luther H. North was commissioned by Gen. Augur, the Dept. Commander, and served as Quarter Master using the name Frank North as Major and the name Luther H. North as Capt., but commissions do not appear on army list.[309]

[309]Christopher C. Augur. Born in N.Y. USMA 1839. 2nd Lt. 2nd Inf. 1 July 1843, 1st Lt. 4th Inf. 12 Nov. 1847, Capt. 1 Aug. 1852, Maj 13th Inf. 14 May 1861. Brigadier General Volunteers 12 Nov. 1861. Maj. Gen. Volunteers for service at Cedar Mountain. Col. 12th Inf. 15 May 1866. Brigadier General USA 4 May 1869. Died 6 Jan. 1898. Powell, *List of Officers*, p. 168.

163

Camp on Custer

Frank's biography was published in the Columbus newspaper (Later will look up date—Camp).

Frank born in 1840 (March 10). The family came from New York State near Ludlowville, Tompkins County, near Ithaca.

Luther born in Richland County, Ohio, place called Plymouth, on March 6, 1846.

In the spring of 1856 the family moved to Nebraska inside what is now the city limits of Omaha. The Pawnees were on a reservation on the south side of the Platte River and a little west of Fremont. In 1859 they moved to near the reservation on the Loup River at Genoa. The Norths lived on a farm above Columbus.

Frank then clerked in a trading post for a man named Rudy. About 1864 Frank went out with Pawnee scouts with General Sam Curtis. Post interpreter McFadden also went along. At the time the Pawnees were not enlisted.[310]

When Curtis got out to the Republican River he turned the command over to General Mitchell and went to Ft. Riley taking 2 Pawnees and Frank with him. From here he instructed Frank to go back to the reservation and

---

[310] This was in August, 1864. General Curtis (on his way to Ft. Kearny to organize an expedition against the hostiles) originated the idea of using as scouts the Indians who were friendly to the whites. Joseph McFadden was a clerk in the Pawnee Agency's trader store. Curtis took him along and made McFadden a captain and Frank North a Lieutenant. Donald F. Danker, *Man of the Plains* (Lincoln: University of Nebraska Press, 1961), p. 29. Luther is half right, the Pawnees were not formally enlisted, but 70 of their number agreed to go along and they campaigned with the troops until the soldiers went into winter quarters. Fairfax Downey, *The Red Blue Coats* (Ft. Collins: Old Army Press, 1973), pp. 31-33. Samuel Curtis. Born Ohio. USMA 1827. 2nd Lt. 7th Inf. 1 July 1831. Resigned 30 June 1832. Col. 3rd Ohio Inf. 23 June 1846. Discharged 24 June 1847. Col. 2nd Iowa Inf. 1, June 1861. Brigadier General U.S.V. 17 May 1861. Maj. Gen. U.S.V. 21 March 1862. Mustered out 30 April 1866. Died 26 Dec. 1866. Francis B. Heitman, *Historical Register and Dictionary of U.S. Army* (Washington: G.P.O., 1903), p. 347.

Interview with Luther H. North

enlist some Pawnee scouts. This he did that winter and started out in spring of 1865. His 1st. Lt. was Jim Murie. All these three officers had regular commissions from the state.[311] Frank was out all that year, including the trip with General Connor, coming back in the late fall of 1865 and wintered.[312]

In the spring of 1866 Frank was appointed trader at Genoa. In the winter of 1866-67 he organized 4 companies of 50 Pawnees each with 1 Capt., 1 Lt. and 1 Sgt. each (white officers). Luther North was one of these Captains (D Company).[313]

We went to Ft. Kearny and got our outfit and put in a good deal of time that summer guarding Union Pacific Railroad construction.

General Augur came along with an expedition and took me and my company and Chas. Morse and his company and Frank as Major and went out in Colorado.[314]

We went up the South Platte, Gen. Sherman was with us, and went north from about where Greeley now is and on north to Cheyenne Pass. Here some men were grading and we camped there and guarded them. The track laying

---

[311]See Danker, *Man of the Plains*, p. 30, for the details of this commission. Territorial Governor Alvin Saunders personally signed Frank's commission on Oct. 24, 1864. Patrick Edward Conner. Born Ireland. Col. 3 Calif. Inf. 4 Sept. 1861. Brigadier General U.S.V. 30 May 1863. Bvt. Maj. Gen. for gallant and meritorious service. Mustered out 30 Apr. 1866. Died 17 Dec. 1891. Heitmann, *Historical Register*, p. 322. Robert B. Mitchell (1823-1882). Moved in 1855 from Ohio to Kansas where he held various political offices. Appointed Col. of 2nd Kansas Inf. Promoted to Brigadier General and assigned to Dept. of Kansas in 1864. In 1865 he was appointed Governor of the New Mexico Territory by President Andrew Johnson. Powell, *List of Officers*, p. 486.

[312]For a good account of Frank North's Pawnees in Connor's Powder River Expedition and the action on the Tongue River, see Downey, *The Red Blue Coats*, pp. 32-33.

[313]This was in March 1867. By the direction of General C. C. Augur, Frank was permitted to appoint his own officers. Danker, *Man of the Plains*, p. 48.

[314]Charles E. Morse (1840-1903) was born in N.Y. and his family moved to Illinois in the 1840s. About 1859 he went to California, but later returned and settled in Columbus, Neb.

at this time had reached only to Sidney. Later we went up to Ft. Laramie with Augur, just my own company with Frank as Maj. When my company got back to Ft. Kearny all the companies were mustered out.

Augur went on to the Powder River country in the fall and took my company of scouts along. Morse and his company went back to Kearny (Frank was Major of the battalion. Ed Arnold was Capt. of A, Morse, Capt. of B, Luther North Capt. of D and Jim Murie Capt. of C).[315]

In the summer of 1867 Frank had a fight with the Cheyennes at Plum Creek (Plum Creek Station at the mouth of Plum Creek, now Lexington). He killed 7 Cheyennes and captured 30 horses and Turkey Legs' wife. Spotted Tail was then camped where North Platte now is.[316]

Sheridan and Augur came out to have a council with Spotted Tail who was then camped at North Platte.[317] They sent for Frank, and when he went into Spotted Tail's tent, Turkey Legs recognized him and said: "Are you not the man I fought with a few days ago at Plum Creek" and Frank said, yes. Then Turkey Legs said, you have my wife and a boy captured, and Frank said yes, and Turkey Legs then said let us exchange prisoners for I have 2 girls and 3 boys and when Frank consented, Turkey Legs started off on a run and brought the children.

The girls were the Martin girls and the boys were also

---

[315] Albert Arnold (1831-1916). The Arnold and North families were very close. They were neighbors both in Florence and in Platte County. Arnold was a member of the Nebraska State Legislature in 1873. James Murie was married to a Pawnee woman, had emigrated from Scotland. He died in the Grand Island, Neb., Soldiers Home.

[316] For the details of this fight, see Thomas W. Dunlay, *Wolves for the Blue Soldiers* (Lincoln: University of Nebraska Press, 1982), pp. 86-87. Another account has 17 warriors killed and a woman, a boy, and a girl captured. Danker, *Man of the Plains*, p. 59.

[317] This was General William T. Sherman, not Sheridan. The meeting was held at North Platte on September 21, 1867. Vestal, *Warpath and Council Fire*, pp. 115-16.

Interview with Luther H. North

white. The Cheyenne boy that Frank exchanged now lives at Lamedeer and is called "Pawnee."[318]

In 1868 I was a clerk for my brother, J. E. North, at Genoa, who then was a trader, he succeeding Frank there as trader.[319]

This year only 2 Companies of Pawnees were enlisted under C. C. Morse and Fred Matthews and Frank as Maj. still.[320]

This year the Pawnee scouts guarded different parts of the railroad construction. Charlie camped at Plum Creek awhile. The companies were split up and distributed along the road.[321]

Frank and Chas. Morse took one company and went south with the Pawnees on their annual buffalo hunt. This was in July. They got into a fight with the Sioux. Frank and Capt. Morse and 7 Pawnees were surrounded in a washout about 6 hours, south of the Republican somewhere. The main body of Pawnees had gone off on a hunt when the Sioux attacked the women in the village and killed a few women.

---

[318]Luther confused this event with the raid of 1864 near Grand Island. This raid involved the Martin family.

These girls were the daughters of Peter Campbell who lived near the present town of Doniphan, Nebraska. They were captured along with their twin brothers on July 24, 1867. John R. Campbell, "The Indian Raid of 1867," *Nebraska State Historical Society Collection*, vol. 17, 1913, pp. 254-62.

[319]James E. North (1838-1913) was the oldest brother. He traded with the Pawnees and was later in the real estate business in Columbus. He served as Sheriff of Platte County, Mayor of Columbus and State Senator. In 1886 he ran for governor on the Democratic ticket but was defeated.

[320]Frederick Matthews (1831-1890) was a Canadian by birth. He drove a stage coach during the years 1864-1866. After his service with the Pawnees, he joined Buffalo Bill's Wild West Show, being the driver of the stage coach which was attacked by Indians. Don Russell, *The Lives and Legends of Buffalo Bill* (Norman: University of Oklahoma Press, 1973), p. 294.

[321]"With Major North's Pawnee Battalion...looking out for the interests of the Union Pacific, it is no wonder hostile Indians, while always a dangerous annoyance, were never a true threat." John Hoyt Williams, *A Great and Shining Road* (N.Y: Time Books, 1988), p. 125.

Camp on Custer

The party with Frank got into a washout, but had little ammunition. One Indian among the Sioux who were fighting Frank was carrying an American flag and he was killed. After that the Indians acted timidly. As soon as the Sioux attacked the village, the scattered Pawnee hunters gathered and drove the Sioux away from the village.

At the washout, all the horses of Frank's party were killed. The Sioux kept increasing until there were about 100 of them. One of the Pawnees was killed in this fight, he being at a distance and was cut off before he could reach Frank and his party.[322]

In the spring of 1869, in February, we enlisted two companies of Pawnees. I was Capt. of Company A and Matthews Capt. of Company B and Frank the Major.

When we got to Ft. McPherson I was ordered down to the Republican to meet Maj. Noyes and Frank was ordered back to enlist one more company of Pawnees.[323] I met Noyes with two troops of cavalry coming north, out of supplies and a big snow storm and blizzard came up and we had a terrible time. Noyes had good horses and went on, but my horses gave out and I had to stop and camp. Noyes camped on Frenchman's Fork of the Republican about a mile from me. He was in the open and he had many horses and mules die that night. One of my men found a canyon with timber and good shelter. We put up poles and made a teepee with a wagon cover. My horses had good shelter and I lost none while Noyes who

---

[322] For an entire chapter devoted to this fight, which is neatly summarized here, see George B. Grinnell, *Two Great Scouts and their Pawnee Battalions* (Lincoln: University of Nebraska Press, 1973), pp. 153-161.

[323] A winter campaign was planned in Feb. 1869 into the Republican River Country to search out hostile villages. Ibid, p. 177. Henry W. Noyes was born in Maine and appointed to West Point. He was made Brevet Major of the Second Cavalry in 1865. Thomas Hammersly, *Complete Regular Army Register* (Washington, D.C: 1880), p. 668.

Interview with Luther H. North

camped only a mile from me in the open, lost many horses and mules. He burnt up his wagons, but about 40 of his men were so frosted that night that when we got to McPherson 3 days later, they had to have surgical attention and some amputations.[324] We built a fire in the teepee and kept warm.

We camped at McPherson a month or so and moved over to North Platte. While we were camped here, Carr came up from the south with the 5th Cavalry and this is the first time I saw Bill Cody.[325]

Carr went east from McPherson and on the Republican 7 Cheyenne dashed into our camp one evening about sundown, and ran off our herd of mules and killed 2 men.[326] We chased them and got the mules back, but did not get the Indians. We now went south to Solomon and when coming back from there, northwest to the Republican, Frank and the 3rd Company under Murie met us before we got to the Republican.[327] We now started up the Republican and found trails everywhere that led nowhere. Up on the Republican, the cavalry camped one night on the south side of the river and we (Pawnee Scouts) on the north side about a ½ mile downstream. This night about a half dozen Cheyennes made a dash

---

[324] No sooner than the command left Ft. McPherson, a blizzard blew up. They got no further than John Burke's ranch when Major Noyes decided to abandon the mission and return to the fort. Grinnell, *Two Great Scouts*, pp. 178-180.

[325] The scouts moved over to North Platte on April 20, 1869. Danker, *Man of the Plains*, p. 99.

[326] The expedition started on June 8th. On June 15th about 5 P.M. the Indians tried to run off the stock. The two men were not killed, only wounded. Privates E. C. Bean of H and C. E. Elwood of M Companies. George F. Price, *Across the Continent with the Fifth Cavalry* (N.Y.: Antiquarian Press, 1959), p. 136, p. 658.

[327] "On June 8th, the day the expedition was to start," Major North was asked to raise a third company. He acted quickly, for he mustered it two days later and joined General Carr in the field with Company C on June 17th. Russell, *Lives and Legends*, p. 126.

and tried to stampede our horses, right in our camp; but the horses were tied and we lost none.[328]

The next day Billy Harvey, M.C. Creede (He afterward discovered the Creede silver mines and sold to David Moffat for 1¼ million. Creede was my Lt.)[329] and I took 6 or 8 Pawnee scouts and went up the Republican about 20 miles, and while we were preparing to go into camp, one of our scouts went up onto a hill and made signs that he saw something. I went up and found we were less than 600 feet from a big Cheyenne crowd going into camp on a little creek.[330] We rode back to camp that night and the next day (July 7) took the trail and followed it to Summit Springs where we struck the village on July 11.

In following the trail, they split so many times we lost much time.

On the morning of the fight, Frank and I had started ahead with the 35 picked Pawnees. We were going north from the Republican to the Platte and the trail split, one branch going northwest and another north and another northeast. Royall with Cody followed the one to the northeast. Frank and I with Pawnees followed the north trail and Carr with 2 Companies of troops and a half dozen Pawnees took the northwest trail. Carr's Pawnees found the village and rode across to us and told us that they had discovered the village. Royall and Cody kept on and when they charged the village they were 15 miles away and we were sent for.[331]

---

[328] This attempt to stampede the horses occurred on July 8th. It occurred about midnight. Danker, *Man of the Plains*, p. 111.

[329] Bill Harvey was a lieutenant in Company A.

[330] This agrees with the field diary kept by Frank North for June 7-11. Donald F. Danker, "The Journal of an Indian Fighter," *Nebraska History*, June 1958, Vol. 39, #2, pp. 137-38.

[331] In Carr's report of the battle, he gives credit to the Pawnees for finding the village. *Report of Operations*, June 30, 1869, to July 20, 1869, NARS, RG 98. However, Don Russell gives the credit to Buffalo Bill. Russell, *The Lives and Legends*, p. 148. Vestal agrees with

Interview with Luther H. North

We rode over to Carr 6 or 7 miles as fast as we could go and Carr consulted Frank as to whether they had better attack with the two companies or wait to bring up Royall. Frank advised attacking right away for fear the Indians might discover us and get away. So Carr decided to charge. We were 3 miles from the village. We charged west toward the village over rolling ground and struck it near the southwest end at 2 p.m.[332] I, Cushing, and Frank with the Pawnees charged ahead into and through village and Carr with 2 companies turned around and charged along the north side of it, from the northwest to southeast, back to the spring.[333] The village was along the brook from the southeast to northwest [see sketch page 172].

The first lodge we struck was Tall Bull's lodge (Cushing had succeeded Murie as Capt. of 3rd Company and Murie at this time was in an ambulance).[334]

Other Indians put up a fight and we dismounted and after firing awhile, the Indians broke and ran and we followed. Before running off, Tall Bull shot the white woman who fell into our hands. She was shot through the breast.[335] We captured 4 women and 14 children prisoners, one of them Tall Bull's wife.

Luther North, the Pawnees found the village. Royall and Cody were sent off on the right hand trail and were too far away to have discovered the village. Vestal, *Warpath and Council Fire*, p. 170.

[332]Carr placed his leading three companies in parallel columns of two and advanced upon the village. It was close to 3 P.M. when the charge was ordered. Fred H. Werner, *The Summit Springs Battle* (Greeley: Werner Publications, 1991), pp. 27-28.

[333]"The Pawnees were all over the village wreaking vengeance on their ancient enemy." James T. King, *War Eagle* (Lincoln: University of Nebraska Press, 1963), p. 113.

[334]Sylvanus E. Cushing (1835-1904) was North's brother-in-law having married Sarah E. North. He was Captain of Company B. Tall Bull's lodge stood to the southwest of the village and as North said, was among the first ones struck. Richard Weingardt, *Sound the Charge* (Englewood: Jacqueline Enterprises, 1978), p. 175.

[335]This was Maria Weichell who had recently immigrated from Germany with her husband George. He was killed at the time of her capture on May 30, 1869. For further details see Weingardt, *Sound the Charge*, pp. 29-30.

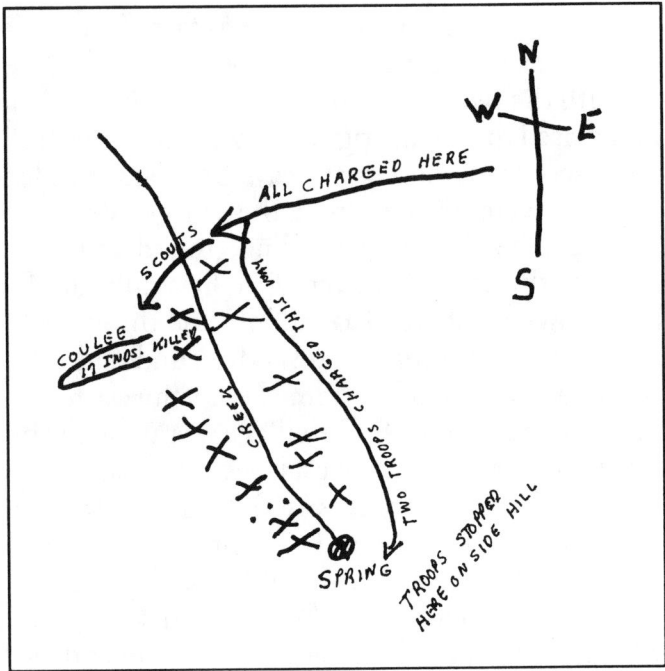

Camp's map of Summit Springs drawn during the North interview.

The Springs run off toward the northwest and sink. They run toward the Platte and sink into the sands. West of the springs, 200 or 300 yards (Springs run from the southeast to northwest) was a small wash or coulee about 15' deep into which ran 17 Indians. One of these was Tall Bull. We killed all of them including some women the Pawnees killed there.[336] All this time the soldiers had

---

[336]It is without a doubt that the Pawnees fought well and hard at Summit Springs. They were riding bareback and reached the village ahead of the soldiers. Grinnell, *Two Great Scouts*, p. 195. As many of the Cheyennes could not reach their horses, they retreated on foot to the nearest ravines. "...the scouts would run up to the canyon, push their guns over the edge, shoot and run back." Ibid, p. 200. After the fight, 19 dead warriors were found.

Interview with Luther H. North

gone on toward the springs as though to surround the village and they followed after the Indians who ran to the south and southwest.

The village was from the springs along the creek 1½ or ¾ miles long on both sides of the creek, strung along. One of my men, Traveling Bear, went into this coulee from the mouth and killed 4 of the Cheyenne and got a Medal of Honor for it.[337]

The rest of the Cheyenne in the coulee were killed from the sides. We were fighting these Indians in the coulee for perhaps an hour. The troops went along the side of the village to the other end.

As we were going along this coulee, an Indian rose up to fire and then dodged back. We stopped and waited for him to rise up again, and Frank suggested that if we would go on, the Indian would rise up again as soon as he would hear the noise of our horses' hoofs. So we started on and Frank (personally) remained with his gun drawn and the instant the Indian rose to fire at me, Frank shot him dead. This was Tall Bull.[338]

Just about that time a squaw climbed up out of the

---

[337] "...and one Pawnee received the Medal of Honor." The name on the citation was that of Sergeant Mad Bear, cited for riding out after a raiding party on July 8th, and being wounded and his horse killed by "friendly fire." Luther North later insisted that the medal was intended for Traveling Bear for bravery at Summit Springs and that the latter actually received the medal. Dunlay, *Wolves for the Blue Soldiers*, p. 158.

[338] There is a tremendous amount of literature about who killed Tall Bull. North said he did, Cody claimed it was he. Each has had his champions and both can bring out an impressive array of witnesses. Don Russell devoted ten pages in his book on Buffalo Bill to analyzing each of the claims and concluded that it was indeed Cody who had shot Tall Bull. Russell, *The Lives and Legends of Buffalo Bill*, pp. 138-48. Grinnell and Danker support Frank North and are just as vehement. Grinnell, *Two Great Scouts*, pp. 199-201 and Danker, *Man of the Plains*, pp. 116-19.

However, none of the accounts in Cody's favor mention a letter Luther wrote to his brother, J.C. North, on Nov. 24, 1874, saying "that big brother of mine killed the chief." It wasn't until 1879 that Buffalo Bill first published his claim regarding Tall Bull. King, *War Eagle*, pp. 114-15. I would be inclined to believe the Norths in regard to Tall Bull's death.

Camp on Custer

coulee, with a child and came running to us with her hand outstretched, and we motioned for her to go to the teepee where we had left the wounded white woman, and she did so. Afterwards this proved to be Tall Bull's wife.[339]

The Indians in the coulee were armed with arrows and some had pistols. They fought to the last and were all killed, most of them at the upper end.[340]

Over at Ft. Sedgwick we had an interview with the Indian woman captive. Leo Palliday was the interpreter and he said after talking a bit, "why one of these women is Tall Bull's wife." We then asked her who killed Tall Bull and she pointed to Frank.

She was captured at the coulee with a little girl.

When we charged into the village, Cushing stopped in a teepee to get a drink of water out of a keg and the wounded white woman ran up and grabbed hold of him almost frightening him to death. She afterwards said Tall Bull in person had shot her.

The other white woman had been killed by some Indian when the Indians ran out of the village. She had been struck in the head with a hatchet or like instrument.[341]

In the village we found about $600 in gold coin and gave it all to the wounded woman, who afterwards married a soldier.[342]

---

[339] This is similar to what Major Carr reported on the capture of Tall Bull's wife. Ibid, p. 113.

[340] "The canyon was about twenty feet deep here and very narrow with perpendicular sides, and many Cheyenne warriors had run up there. They were armed with bows and arrows and when anyone came within sight near the canyon, they let fly their arrows." Grinnell, *Two Great Scouts*, p. 199.

[341] Susanna Alderdice was buried on the field at Summit Springs. Her husband, Thomas, survived as he was at Salina, Kansas, on that day. Weingardt, *Sound the Charge*, p. 32.

[342] Maria Weichall survived her wound and married the hospital Steward who took care of her at Ft. Sedgwick. Danker, *Man of the Plains*, p. 119.

Interview with Luther H. North

The Indians were pursued from the village in different directions and some killed at some distance from the village. We rounded up about 400 horses and 120 mules, but Cheyennes got away with a good many of them. Most of the Indians killed were those killed by the Pawnees at the coulee. The official report of Indians killed was exaggerated.[343]

When Royall and Cody got to the village the fight was all over. Ned Buntline (E.C.Z. Judson) afterward at Ft. Sedgwick wrote him up and etc. and he told how he had discovered the village, charged into it, killed Tall Bull, etc., all of which was fiction. Cody took no part in the battle.[344]

After the fight we camped on the site of the village that night and then went to Ft. Sedgwick (Julesburg).[345] About 3 weeks later we started south out of Sedgwick under Royall. I was in charge of Scouts (Frank was not along). We struck the Cheyenne trail and it swung around north and crossed the Platte just above Ogallala. Here Frank met us and took command and I went home. They followed them north but did not catch them.

In 1870 two companies of Pawnees were out. I had one Company (A) and Cushing another (B). We were guard-

---

[343] Frank North recorded in his diary 60 Indians were killed and 17 were made prisoner. Werner, *The Summit Springs Battle*, p. 80. In Carr's official reports he listed 52 Indians killed and 17 women and children captured. Ibid, p. 56. Thus it would seem North's account was the one which overstated the number of Cheyenne killed.

[344] Here is another conflicting statement which North made. Grinnell took at face value that Royall and Cody were not in the battle. Grinnell, *Two Great Scouts*, p. 201. However, as in footnote 331, Royall and Cody were sent to follow up one of the trails, but the detachment returned just as Carr's column was making preparations for the battle. Carr's official report elaborated: "About the time Colonel Royall rejoined with his command, having found that the animals reported were bushes. He had traveled nearly twenty miles through sand." Werner, *The Summit Springs Battle*, p. 64. Luther North could have been busy with his own preparations for battle and simply missed seeing Royall and Cody report back in.

[345] The command reached Fort Sedgwick at noon on July 15, 1869.

Camp on Custer

ing the railroad. I was camped at Plum Creek and Cushing at O'Fallon nearly all summer, but no fighting.

Between 1870 and 1876 there were no Pawnees enlisted until after the Custer fight.

Frank was in service as post guide from '72 to '76 at Ft. D.A. Russell and at Sidney Barricks. From 1870 to '72 he was out of service.

After the Custer fight both of us enlisted 100 Pawnees in Indiana (12 Companies) by command of Sheridan.[346] We marched them 120 miles to Coffeyville, Kansas, and got to Sidney in Sept. and got horses and outfit and thence to Ft. Robinson.

We went out in the night from our camp on a creek somewhere south of Ft. Robinson and took Red Cloud and his village from Chadron Creek or White River to Robinson and they were disarmed. Then we went over to Laramie with 720 head of Red Cloud's horses.[347] The Sioux were disarmed by the troops, not by us. The Pawnees drove the horses to Laramie. We stayed at Laramie until we started for the Powder River. Crook came up to Ft. Laramie and we went on to Ft. Fetterman and thence over to Ft. Reno and thence to Crazy Woman where Crook made camp and sent McKenzie [sic] out to the village where scouts came in and reported the presence of a village.[348]

---

[346]"Sheridan, never an advocate of the use of Indian auxiliaries, had nevertheless called Frank North to Chicago and recruited him and his brother to raise 100 Pawnee scouts for use against the Sioux." Paul A. Hutton, *Phil Sheridan and His Army* (Lincoln: University of Nebraska Press, 1985), p. 323.

[347]This was in October of 1876. Years later an old Sioux told Luther North that the soldiers could not have taken the horses by themselves and in fact had brought the Pawnees along to protect them. Dunlay, *Wolves for the Blue Soldiers*, p. 161.

[348]This was on Nov. 21, 1876. Col. Ranald Slidell Mackenzie with 800 cavalry men and nearly all the Indian scouts, were dispatched to the Big Horn Mountains in search of the Cheyenne. Danker, *Man of the Plains*, p. 211. Col. Mackenzie (1840-1889) was born in

Interview with Luther H. North

We left camp on Crazy Woman one morning and rode all day and all night and struck Dull Knife's camp in the early morning.[349]

Pawnees went into the fight by themselves. We entered the village and McKinney went around it and was killed when he came upon a coulee in which some Indians had taken refuge.[350] This coulee ran from the creek north to the mountain and I was within 100 yards of him when he was killed. We stayed in the village and the Cheyenne fired at us all day from the hills within gunshot. Soldiers scattered all around exchanging shots back and forth with the Cheyenne. Really, the charge on this village was a bungling affair. Perhaps 1,000 men were there and all day long they failed to drive the 200 or so Indians out of the rocks.[351] We burned the village and turned them out into the cold, but did not kill many Indians.[352]

MISCELLANEOUS NOTES

In the Dull Knife fight, says Luther North, when

N.Y.C. and graduated from West Point in 1862. At war's end he was a cavalry division commander, a rise just as spectacular as Custer's. Mackenzie was relieved of command at Ft. Sill so he could take part in the Powder River Expedition with six companies of his 4th Cavalry. He later served in the southwest and was a brigadier general at the time of his death.

[349]This action was the Dull Knife fight. It occurred on Nov. 25, 1876. See Fred H. Werner, *The Dull Knife Battle* (Greeley: Werner Publication, 1981).

[350]This was Lt. John A. McKinney, Company H, 3rd Cavalry. Born in Tenn. USMA 1867. 2nd Lt. 4th Cavalry. 12 June, 1871. 1st Lt. 17 May 1876. Killed 25 Nov. 1876 in action with Indians in Wyoming. Powell, *List of Officers*, p. 471.

[351]One participant stated, "It would have been quite possible for Mackenzie to have inflicted greater punishment on the hostiles, killing more of them, inevitably losing more on our side... but he pushed the engagement so far and then held his ground." James S. McClellan, "The Dull Knife Fight," *Motor Travel Magazine*, Nov. 1930.

This might account for Mackenzie not driving the Indians from their defensive positions. The warriors numbered close to 400, not 300. Werner, *The Dull Knife Battle*, p. 31.

[352]The soldiers lost one officer and 5 enlisted men with 25 men and one scout wounded. The body count of Cheyenne found on the battlefield totaled 25. Brown, *Plainsmen of the Yellowstone*, pp. 299-300.

Camp on Custer

McKinney charged on the gully and was killed, the soldiers all ran back but Ralph Weeks, one of our Pawnees who was educated[353] and spoke good English, who rode up in front of them and cried out: "What are you running for? There are only six or seven Indians in there." In this way the soldiers turned again and attacked the Indians in the gully and followed them up.

Dull Knife Campaign

L. H. North says that after the Dull Knife fight, Crook moved over to the Powder and then up the Fry Fork to the head, and then north to the head of the Belle Fourche River, west of Black Hills.[354] Finding nothing, they then moved back south. While over there they came onto a burning coal mine and he recently heard (1919) that same mine is still afire.

Dull Knife Fight

Luther North says the ground was entirely bare that day of the fight. The snow fell that night. I asked him particularly about this on December 17, 1919.[355]

Crook's Discipline

Capt. L. H. North says that Crook's campaigns which

---

[353] Ralph Weeks was educated at Carlisle Indian School. He later went to Oklahoma and studied law and became quite prominent in the early days of that state. "One of our sergeants (Ralph Weeks) in the Dull Knife fight counted coup on a live Cheyenne youth, who was hiding in a clump of bushes, then killed and scalped him." Robert Bruce, *The Fighting Norths and Pawnee Scouts* (N.Y.:n.p., 1932), p. 20.

[354] This was December 10, 1876. For a detailed account of North's activities after the Dull Knife Campaign, see Danker, *Man of the Plains*, pp. 219-25.

[355] This is correct; the ground was bare on the day of the battle. "During the night (Nov. 25) a heavy snow began and by morning the ground was covered with five or six inches of snow." Grinnell, *Two Great Scouts*, p. 274.

Interview with Luther H. North

he participated in were conducted in the most slipshod manner.[356] For illustration, he says that on the way to the Powder River in the Fall of 1876, his command moved out and was going up the Platte one day, Crook selected a convenient camping place for himself and an escort of a company of cavalry. The others came along and marched on past 8 or 10 miles and camped where they pleased and the wagon train did not get up at all, coming along the next day without an escort. In the morning each part of the command moved pretty much as it pleased, without orders.[357]

On the way back from the Dull Knife Fight we went up to the Dry Fork of the Powder about to the head. The Pawnee scouts were instructed to camp in a very exposed place on the bald face of a hill, where it was extremely cold.

It was not his habit to send the adjutant around the night before with marching orders for the following day. The next morning the scouts packed up early and stood in the cold a long while waiting for the order to march, while the cavalry stood ready to mount, knocking their heels to keep warm and after remaining in such condition for an hour or more, the orders came that they would not move that day. The next morning the same performance was repeated.

While in camp at Ft. Laramie a big snow storm came up and there had been no orders about moving, until suddenly one morning Capt. Clark came along and peeked into our tent and said: "You fellows had better get busy—

---

[356]For a full length biography of Crook, see Martin F. Schmitt, *General George Crook* (Norman: University of Oklahoma Press, 1964).

[357]For another instance of Crook's inaction and sloppiness, see Danker, *Man of the Plains*, pp. 210, 218-219.

the command is moving."³⁵⁸ North says that actually the whole command had been packed up and ordered to move without informing them that they were to move that day. Says Crook's movement all along was in just that reckless manner.

BATTLE OF WHITE STONE HILLS

Enlisted in the fall of 1862 in 2nd Nebraska Volunteer Cavalry. We quartered that winter at Genoa on Pawnee reservation, 20 miles up the Loup River from Columbus. In Spring of 1863 we went over to Sioux City and joined Sully who had the 6th Iowa Cavalry.³⁵⁹ He took both regiments up the Missouri to old Ft. Pierre and from here we went east. Sibley was coming out from Minnesota and Sully intended to join him.³⁶⁰ Sibley followed the Indians to the Missouri River. They crossed and Sibley started back east and we never did meet him. When he started east, the Indians followed him and attacked him several times and harassed him. He burned some of his wagons.

We followed the Indians and overtook them and they broke camp and tried to get away. We had 8 companies of 2nd Nebraska Cavalry and the full regiment of the 6th Iowa Cavalry, perhaps 1,200 or 1,500 men. Our regiment

---

[358] This was Lt. William P. Clarke, Company F, Second Cavalry. He was detailed as an aide to Crook on 21 Aug. 1876. He was born in N.Y. USMA 1864, 2nd Lt. 2nd Cav. 15 June 1865. 1st Lt. 10 July 1869. Adj. 31 July 1869 to 1 July 1876. Capt. 25 Jan. 1881. Died 22 Sept. 1884. Powell, *List of Officers*, p. 245.

[359] For a full length biography of Alfred Sully, see Langdon Sully, *No Tears for the General* (Palo Alto: Am. West Pub. Co., 1974). He was born in Pa. 2nd Lt. 2nd Inf. 1 July 1841. 1st Lt. 11 Mar. 1847, Capt.. 23 Feb. 1852, Col. 1st Minn. Vol. 4 March 1862, Bvt. Brig. Gen. U.S.V. 12 March 1865 for gallant and meritorious service in campaign against the Indians in the northwest and in the battle of White Stone Hill, Dak. Lt. Col. 3rd Inf. 28 July 1866. Col. 21st Inf. 10 Dec. 1873. Died 27 April 1879. Powell, *List of Officers*, p. 615.

[360] Henry Hastings Sibley (1811-1891). Born Michigan. Brig. Gen. U.S.V. 29 Sept. 1862. Bvt. Maj. Gen. U.S.V. 29 Nov. 1865 for efficient and meritorious service. Mustered out 30 April 1866. He was later active in banking and commerce. He died on 13 Feb. 1891. Powell, *List of Officers*, p. 886.

Interview with Luther H. North

dismounted and struck the Indian camp in a semicircle and the 6th Iowa attacked the camp mounted from the other side and the Indians ran right into the 6th Iowa. There must have been about 3,000 Indians there. We camped near there on a lake for two or three days after this fight. The fight was on Sept. 3, 1863.[361]

We captured 156 prisoners, men, women, and children. We went right back to Ft. Pierre taking these prisoners with us and there split up. Two of our companies went down to Crow Creek Agency where there were a lot of Santee squaws that had been in the Minnesota massacre the year before....

Miscellaneous Notes

INQ. Lute North: Discuss with him again attack in Arapahoe Camp. How near he went to Yellowstone and where came on the track of Cole, where wagons burned and where he overtook Cole?[362]

Was not with expedition in 1865 at all.[363]

Did he ever serve with Delaware scouts, where and who?

No.

INQ. Luther North
Indian names for Frank and Luther North.
Frank—Pawnee *Leshor* (Chief)
Luther—*Leshor Kittipats* (Chief) (Little)

---

[361] For a long account of the battle, see Sully, *No Tears for the General*, pp. 172-178. Also, see A. N. Judd, *Campaigning Against the Sioux* (N.Y: John M. Carroll & Company, 1973).

[362] For a good account of Col. Nelson Cole's expedition of June 1865 see Fred B. Rogers, *Soldiers of the Overland* (San Francisco: The Grabhorn Press, 1938).

[363] Luther North might not have been on this expedition, but his brother Frank and their Pawnees helped secure and guide the troops back to civilization after they ran out of rations in September and were hopelessly lost. Donald Danker, *Man of the Plains* (Lincoln: University of Nebraska Press, 1961), p. 33.

Camp on Custer

Pawnees always dressed in blue uniforms, like soldiers, all the time they served as enlisted scouts, says Luther North.

Logan Foutanelle, Chief of the Omahas, was killed in the '50s by the Sioux, says L. H. North. He says, however, he had heard it disputed in later years that he died a natural death, but thinks the former the correct opinion as it was currently repeated that he was killed.

Ft. Kearny was on south side of Platte, some 3 or 4 miles below where the town is now.

Plum Creek stage station was on the south side of the Platte. Three or 4 miles this side of the present town of Lexington. The Plum Creek station of the railroad was also some 3 or 4 miles this side of Lexington. The old Overland trail cut across from St. Joe and Ft. Kearny and all the early trails were on the south side of the Platte.

Index

American Horse: 136
Arnold, Albert: 166
Augur, Brig. Gen. Christopher C: 163, 165

Bach, Lt. Col. C. A: 23-24
Bad Gun: 131
Bailey, John A. (E.): 35, 61; interview with, 81-84
Baker, Maj. Eugene M: 51
Baliran, Augustus: 40, 54-55, 99; death of, 41-42
Ball, John H: 42n
Battle of Whitestone Hills: 180-81
Bear's Ears: 58n
Benteen, Capt. Frederick W: 35, 39n, 54n, 73, 156-57; overhears Reno and Weir conversation, 94-95
Bernard, Joe: 40
Bighorn River: 55
Big Road: 121
Black Crow: 117
Black Elk: 150n
Black Moon: 90
Bloody Knife: 42, 44n, 45, 58, 109, 128; kills Medicine Man, 43
Bobtail Bull: 129
Bordeaux, Louis: in death of Crazy Horse, 133-37; interview with 137-51; argues with Grouard 140, 144-45; describes death of Crazy Horse, 149-50; describes Crazy Horse, 151
Bourke, Lt. John G: 151n
Bouyer, Mitch: 83-84, 89
Botzer, Edward: 75-76
Braden, Lt. Charles: 49, 50n, 55
Bradley, Lt. James H: 114
Bradley, Lt. Col. Luther P: 140n, 145-46
Brave Bear: 100; hung, 102
Bridger, James: 36
Brigham Young University: 27
Brisbin, Maj. James S: 82-83
Brown, Alexander: 75-76
Brown, Brig. Gen. William C: 13, 19, 20n, 21-26, 22 (portrait); turns over "Camp Notes" to Ellison, 27
Bruguier, John: 100-102; interview with, 87-91; biog. of, 87-88
Bruguier, Samuel: 91, 104n; on capture of Rain In The Face, 99-102; biog. of, 99; on the Bozeman Fight, 103-104
Buntline, Ned: 175
Burke, Capt. Daniel W: 142, 144
Burkman, John: interview with, 120; biog. of, 119
Butler, James: 113

Camp on Custer

Calhoun, Lt. James: 44n, 53, 59n
Callan, Thomas J: 82, 111
Callahan, John J: 106
Camp Robinson: 140n, 141, 145
Camp Sheridan: 138, 142
Camp, Emeline: 21, 24-25; sells husband's collection, 26
Camp, Walter M: 13-28, 107n, 113, 114n, 118n; portrait, 2, 16; early life, 14-15; method of interviewing, 17-18; friendship with Ellison, 19-20; death of, 21; distribution of papers, 27-28
Carr, Maj. Eugene A: 169
Casselberry, J. R: 100
Chapman, William E: 83
Charley, Vincent: 96-97, 98n; death of, 98
Chips: 127, 136
Clark, Benjamin: 36n
Clark, Lt. William P: 126, 135, 138, 141n, 150n; reaction to Crazy Horse's death, 150
Clarke, Lt. William P: 179
Clear, Elihu: 74
Clement, Basil: 45n, 50n
Cody, William F: 169-70, 173n, 175; claim of killing Tall Bull disputed, 175
Cole, Col. Nelson: 181
Coleman, Thomas W: 82, 112; member of water party, 109-10
Comanche: 156, 158 (portrait), 162; discovery by Kennedy, 159; not with *Far West*, 159-60

Conner, Maj. Gen. Patrick E: 165
Cooke, Lt. William W: 92
Corbin, Jack: 36n
Crazy Horse: 114-15, 124, 126-27; Bordeaux's notes and interview on death, 133-51; Grouard misinterprets, 140; stabbed by guard, 147-48; death, 149-50; burial, 150; meaning of name, 151
Creede, M.C: 170
Criswell, Benjamin C: 34, 60
Crook, Brig. Gen. George: 125, 137n, 147n, 176, 178, 180; criticized by North, 179-80
Cross, Billy: 88-89, 90n
Crow Breast: 131
Crow Creek Agency: 181
Crow Dog: killing of Spotted Tail, 117
Crows Nest: 127
Cunningham, John: 57n
Curtis, Brig. Gen. Samuel: 164
Cushing, Sylvanus E: 171, 174-75
Custer Battlefield National Monument (Little Bighorn Battlefield National Monument): 27
Custer City, S.D: 58-59
Custer, Boston: 81, 113
Custer, Elizabeth B: 15, 38, 40
Custer, Lt. Col. George A: 17, 34, 57 (portrait), 72, 74, 77-78, 81, 94, 100, 123, 127-28, 156; reason not scalped, 35;

Index

Washita Battle, 36-37; Yellowstone Expedition, 37-55; Black Hills Expedition, 56-61
Custer, Capt. Thomas W: 47, 49, 87, 106, 113; captures Rain-In-The-Face, 101-102

Dale, Alfred W: interview with, 105-106; biog., of 105
Dandy: 92, 120
Denver Public Library: 27-28
DeRudio, Lt. Charles C: 91
Donaldson, Aris B: 56n, 57n, 58n
Dose, Henry C: 77
Dorman, Isaiah: 101
Dull Knife: 177-79

Edgerly, Lt. Winfield S: 65, 96-97, 123n, 161; at Weir Point, 97-98
11th Kansas Cavalry: 20-21, 23
Ellison, Robert S: 13, 19 (portrait), 21-25; receives "Camp Notes" from Brown, 26-27; death of, 27; collection disposed of, 27-28

Far West: 93, 106
Fehler, Henry: 92
Ferguson, Rev. Robert: 22
Fight at Crow Butte: 133
Foley, John: 124n
Foolish Bear: 130
Forked Horn: 129
Forts: Abraham Lincoln, 52, 56n, 58, 94, 107, 129n; Buford, 114; D.A. Russell, 176; Fetterman, 176; Kearny, 182; Keogh, 82, 88, 104, 113, 155; Laramie 146, 176, 179; McPherson, 168-69; Pierre, 180-81; Randall, 67-68; Reno, 176; Rice, 38; Robinson, 115, illus. of, 141, 176; Sedgwick, 174-75
Foutanelle, Logan: 182
Fox, John: biog. of, 94; interview with, 94-96

Gaffney, George: biog. of, 93; interview with, 93-94
Gall: 103, 123n
Garnett, William: 138n, 146n, 149n
Garnier, Baptiste: death of, 115
"Garry Owen": 37, 46
Gentles, William: 136n
Gerard, Frederick: 78, 113
Gilbert, Col. Charles C: 65-66
Godfrey, Capt. Edward S: 106n, 123n
Goldin, Theodore W: 75, 111
Graham, Col. William A: 18
Grant, Frederick D: 52-53, 54n; on Black Hills Expedition, 56
Gratiot, James: 25-26
Greenleaf Creek: 103-104
Grinnell, George B: 19, 123n
Grouard, Frank: 135-37, 139 (portrait), 144; afraid of Crazy Horse, 139; misinterprets Crazy Horse, 140, 144-45
Guthrie, George: 48

185

Half Yellow Face: 72, 118, 162
Hammer, Dr. Kenneth: 13, 27
Hare, Lt. Luther R: 161
Harrison, Thomas W: biog. of, 97; interview with, 97-98; portrait, 98; witnesses Charley's death, 98
Harvey, William: 170
Henley (Hindley), John: biog. of, 31-33; interviews with, 31-68; portrait, 32; Washita Battle interview, 36-37; Yellowstone Expedition interview, 37-55; Black Hills interview, 56-61; Little Bighorn Battle interview, 61-64; regarding Sitting Bull, 64-68; water party, 109-10
Hodgson, Lt. Benjamin H: 40, 46, 82-83, 161; body found, 81
Honsinger, Dr. John: 40, 55, 99; death of, 41-42
Horn-In-Front: 129
Howe, Capt. Edgar W: 64
Hughes, Francis F: 73, 92, 93n
Hughes, Robert H: 72-73
Hump: 89-90

Johnson, Benjamin: 76

Kanipe, Daniel A: 15
Kellogg, Marcus H: 119
Kennedy, Francis Johnson: biog. of, 153-55; statement regarding Little Bighorn Battle, 155-61; identifies Keogh's body, 160; mutilation of Reno's dead, 160
Kennington, Capt. James: 136, 147n; and killing of Crazy Horse, 147, 149
Keogh, Capt. Myles W: 93, 96, 113, 156, 161 (portrait); body identified by Kennedy, 160
Ketchum, Lt. Hiram H: 47n; destroys whiskey, 54-55
Kill Eagle: 64n, 90
King, Gen. Charles: 22
Korn, Gustave: 74, 83
Kuhlman, Dr. Charles: 27

Lame Deer: 104
Lame White Man: 63n
Lassiter, M.G. William: 23, 25
Lattman, John: biog. of, 75; interview with, 75-80;
Lee, Lt. Jesse M: 142, 144-45, 146, 147n
Lilly Library (University of Indiana): 27
Little Bighorn Battle: 70 (map), 76, 106, 113, 121-25; interview with Henley regarding, 61-64; Camp's notes on, 107-20; Kennedy's statement regarding, 155-62
Little Big Man: 126, 146, 148 (portrait), 149-50; calls Crazy Horse a coward, 147
Lord, Dr. George E: 106

McCarthy, Charles: body identified, 92

Index

McDougall, Capt. Thomas M: 81
McFadden, Joseph: 164
McGillycuddy, Dr. Valentine: 148n, 149n
McIntosh, Lt. Donald: 78; body identified, 80
McKay, William: 59n
McKinney, Lt. John A: 177; death of, 178
McVeigh, David: biog. of, 91; interview with, 91-93
Mackenzie, Col. Ranald S: 176, 177n
Madden, Michael P: 110, 112, 157
Mad Bull: 58n
Marshall, Jasper: 120
Matthews, Frederick: 167-68
Medicine Tail Coulee: 122
Miles, Brig. Gen. Nelson A: 88-89, 104
Morse, Charles E: 165, 167
Moylan, Capt. Myles: 91, 95, 161
Musselshell River: 50

Nez Percé: 140, 141n
New York *Herald*: 119
Noonan (Nash), Mrs. John: 89, 90n
Norris, Gilman: 45n
North Platte River: 166, 172
North, Frank: 163, 165, 169, 171, 181; fight at Plum Creek Station, 166; fight on branch of Republican River, 167-68; advises Carr to attack, 171; kills Tall Bull, 173; Dull Knife fight, 177-79
North, James E: 167
North, Luther H: biog. of, 163; interview with, 163-81; Battle of Summit Springs, 171-74; Dull Knife fight, 177-79; criticism of Crook, 179-80
Noyes, Maj. Henry W: 168

O'Brien, Capt. Lyster M: 64
O'Hara, Miles F: 84 (portrait), 85, 86n
O'Neill, Thomas: 108 (portrait)
One Feather: biog. of, 127; interview with, 127-30
One Stab: 58n

Palliday, Leo: 174
Pandtle, Christopher: 106
Pompey's Pillar: 50-51
Porter, Dr. Henry R: 106
Powder River: 107, 179

Ragsdale, John S: 109
Rain-In-The-Face: 61, 160; capture of, 99-102
Ramsey, Charles: 158
Red Buttes: 19n
Red Cloud: 136, 137n, 138 (portrait), 139n, 176
Red Cloud Agency: 115, 126, 138, 142; illus., 143
Red Star: 127-28
Reno, Maj. Marcus A: 60n, 62-63, 71, 74, 78, 83, 96, 110n,

187

121, 155, 157; argues with Weir, 94
Republican River: 167-68
Reynolds, Charles A: 43-44, 45n, 61, 89; carries news of gold, 60
Robb, Eldorado S: 77
Roller, William: 57n, 58n
Romero: 36n
Ross, Horatio: 59n
Rosser, Thomas L: 38
Roy, Stanislaus: 111-12
Royall, Lt. Col. William B: 170, 175
Running Antelope: 65-66, 91
Rushing Bull (Little Crow): 129-30
Ryder, Hobert: 106

Scott, Gen. Hugh L: 20
2nd Nebraska Cavalry: 180
Seifert, August: biog. of, 71; interview with, 71-74
7th Cavalry: 34, 38-39, 41, 83, 94, 159
7th Infantry: 159
17th Infantry: 64-65
Shave Elk (Thomas Disputed): interview with, 121-27; meaning of name, 125
Sheridan, Lt. Gen. Philip H: 56n, 126n, 147n, 166
Sherman, Lt. Gen. William T: 165
Short, Nathan: 74, 86
Sibley, Brig. Gen. Henry H: 180

Sitting Bull: 34, 61-63, 65 (portrait), 67n, 68n, 88, 102-103, 114, 125n; interview with Henley regarding, 64-68
Sivertsen, John: 110, 111 (portrait)
6th Iowa Cavalry: 180-81
Sniffin, Frank: biog. of, 84-85; interview with, 85-87
Son of the Star: 131
Spinner, Philipp: 82
Spotted Blackbird: 62n
Spotted Tail: biog. of, 116 (portrait); 126, 137-38, 139n, 166; regarding his death, 116-17
Spotted Tail Agency: 142-43, 145
Standing Bear: 146
Standing Rock Agency: 100 (illus.), 113-14
Stanley, Col. David S: 39, 47, 49, 50-53, 54n, 55, 100
Strikes Two: 128
Sully, Brig. Gen. Alfred: 180
Summit Springs: 170; Battle of, 171-74
Swift Bear: 149

Tall Bull: 171, 174; shoots white woman, 171; death of, 173
Taylor, Muggins: 94
Taylor, Walter O: 76
Terry, Brig. Gen. Alfred H: 63, 73n, 86, 106-107, 155, 158
Thomas Disputed: *see* Shave Elk
Thompson, Peter: 86, 97n, 111

Index

Tobey, Maj. Thomas: 147n, 148n
Todd, Tour: possibly stabbed Crazy Horse, 136
Touch The Clouds: 134 (portrait), 135, 145, 149
Traveling Bear: 173
Turkey Legs: 166
Turner, George: 57n, 58n
Tuttle, John H: 49, 50; death of, 46n
22nd Infantry: 38, 53-54, 100
Two Strikes: 134

Van Horne, Capt. William McC: 64
Varden, Frank E: 93
Varnum, Lt. Charles A: 72n
"Vic": 92, 120, 123n
Vickory, John: 72
Voss, Henry: 73, 92n

Wallace, Lt. George D: 161
Wallace, Richard A: drowns on picket duty, 84
Warner, Oscar T: 87
Watson, James: 86
Weaver, George W: 85
Weeks, Ralph: 178
Weir, Capt. Thomas B: 94, 95 (portrait), 96, 97n, 98
"Western": 115
Whitebear, George: 75
White Man Runs Him: 122
White Swan: 71-72; biog. of, 118; Camp's notes on, 118
Whole Buffalo: 129-30
Williams, Dr. John W: 105-106
Winney, Dewitt: 73
Wooden Leg: 16 (portrait), 121n, 124n
Wounded Knee: 74

Yankton, S.D: 37-38
Yellowstone River: 108, 125, 155